THE
SETTLE & CARLISLE LINE

• A PAST and PRESENT COMPANION •

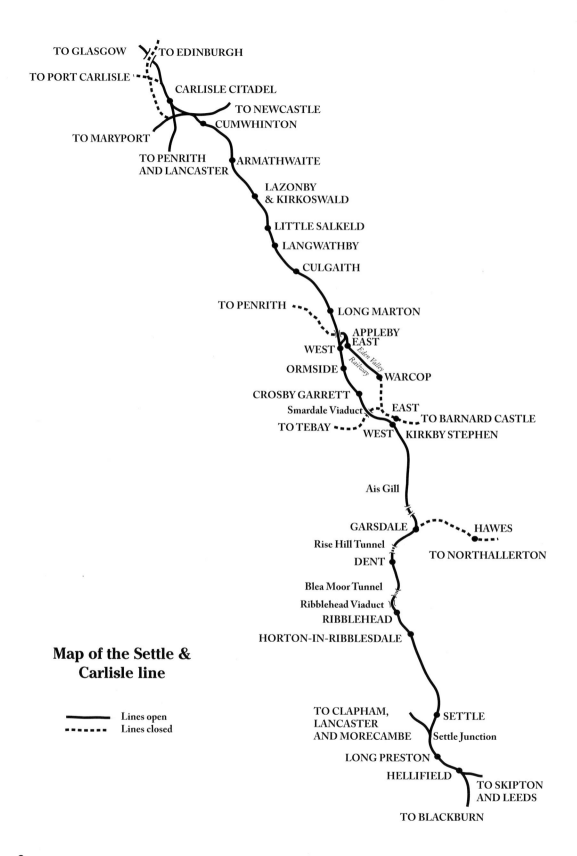

TO GLASGOW TO EDINBURGH

TO PORT CARLISLE

CARLISLE CITADEL

TO NEWCASTLE

CUMWHINTON

TO MARYPORT

TO PENRITH
AND LANCASTER

ARMATHWAITE

LAZONBY
& KIRKOSWALD

LITTLE SALKELD

LANGWATHBY

CULGAITH

TO PENRITH

LONG MARTON

APPLEBY
EAST

WEST

ORMSIDE

Eden Valley Railway

WARCOP

CROSBY GARRETT

Smardale Viaduct

EAST

TO BARNARD CASTLE

TO TEBAY

WEST

KIRKBY STEPHEN

Ais Gill

GARSDALE

HAWES

Rise Hill Tunnel

TO NORTHALLERTON

DENT

Blea Moor Tunnel

Ribblehead Viaduct

RIBBLEHEAD

HORTON-IN-RIBBLESDALE

**Map of the Settle &
Carlisle line**

TO CLAPHAM,
LANCASTER
AND MORECAMBE

SETTLE

Settle Junction

LONG PRESTON

HELLIFIELD

TO SKIPTON
AND LEEDS

TO BLACKBURN

——— Lines open
------- Lines closed

THE
SETTLE & CARLISLE
LINE

∘ A PAST and PRESENT COMPANION ∘

*A nostalgic trip along the whole route
from Hellifield to Carlisle*

David J. Williams

RAILWAY HERITAGE
from
The NOSTALGIA Collection

ISBN 978 1 85895 263 5

Past & Present Publishing Ltd
The Trundle
Ringstead Road
Great Addington
Kettering
Northants NN14 4BW

Tel/Fax: 01536 330588
email: sales@nostalgiacollection.com
Website: www.nostalgiacollection.com

Printed and bound in the Czech Republic

First published in 2010

British Library Cataloguing in Publication Data

A catalogue record for this book is available from the British Library.

ACKNOWLEDGEMENTS

The book has benefited greatly from the involvement and help of a number of photographers, holders of collections and those with valuable historical knowledge. I would like to thank, in strictly alphabetical order, David Adams, Tony Bowles, Richard Casserley, Bob Ellis, Keith Greenwood, David J. Mitchell, Alan Price, Malcolm Ranieri, Derek Soames, David Stacey, Terry Walsh and Tony Whitby. Whether contributing to a single sentence or providing a whole series of pictures, the contribution is very much appreciated.

British Railways 'Britannia' Class 4-6-2 No 70052 *Firth of Tay* is seen at Hellifield with a three-coach local bound for Carlisle in 1965; this locomotive was involved in a fatal accident near Settle in 1960. *David J. Mitchell*

CONTENTS

INTRODUCTION

Over the years, many books have been written on the Settle to Carlisle Railway, so it is perhaps a good starting point to state what this latest book is not. It does not aim to be a complete and comprehensive examination of the line and its history – this has been done before, and often, and in many cases extremely well, by others. Nor does it pretend to be an all-encompassing photographic survey of every signal, brick and structure on the line – this, too, has been done elsewhere, and done very well. The intention in compiling this book is to attempt to illustrate the changes that have taken place over the years on the line, for better or worse, comparing the appearance and nature of the line and its traffic in years gone by with that which can be seen by passengers and visitors today. While doing this, it will hopefully inform readers of just some of the many things to see and do both on and around the line and briefly touch, however inadequately, upon the achievements of those who built it, those who saved it, and those who continue to work for its continued prosperity today.

It is perhaps appropriate to give a basic outline of the history of the line, to put in context what exists today. The Settle to Carlisle route was originally born out of the antagonism and rivalry between the Midland Railway (MR) and the London & North Western Railway (LNWR). In the 1860s, at least in theory, the MR had an excellent route to the North of England, and Scotland, from St Pancras station in London, by way of Derby, Leeds and Carlisle, and from there to Glasgow via the Glasgow & South Western Railway's tracks and to Edinburgh via the 'Waverley' route of the North British Railway (NBR). However, one section of the journey proved a stumbling block – that beyond Ingleton into Carlisle. This stretch of line had been built by the Lancaster & Carlisle Railway and was leased to the LNWR. Moreover, the MR accessed Ingleton via the lines of another company, the

A start of the Settle & Carlisle line, in more ways than one! A London & North Western Railway (LNWR) train arrives at Carlisle Citadel station from the south behind 'Precedent' Class 2-4-0 No 1531 *Cromwell* and 'Experiment' Class 4-6-0 No 261. In the 1860s the LNWR controlled both routes from the south into Carlisle, the main line over Shap Summit (now part of the West Coast Main Line) and the alternative route between Ingleton and Carlisle via Kirkby Lonsdale and Sedburgh, by leasing the line from the Lancaster & Carlisle Railway. It was frustration with the stalled negotiations over better access to the latter route that convinced the Midland Railway that it would have to 'go it alone' to obtain a satisfactory route to Scotland, the solution being a line to Settle, Kirkby Stephen, Appleby and through the Eden Valley to Carlisle. *H. Gordon Tidey, RAS Marketing*

'Little' North Western Railway, which had been incorporated on 26 June 1846, and by 31 July 1849 was running between Skipton and Ingleton, the latter location reached by means of a 4-mile single-line

branch off the 'main line' from Clapham (the line eventually connected Skipton with Morecambe as from 1 June 1850). It was worked by the MR from 1 June 1852, leased from 1 January 1859, and later absorbed by that company. However, once at Ingleton, at the opposite end of the town's viaduct was a rival station, and the line onwards through Kirkby Lonsdale and Sedburgh to Carlisle was leased to the LNWR, which was hostile to MR traffic reaching Scotland with any level of comfort. Therefore the LNWR, with its main line over Shap, controlled both of the existing routes to Carlisle. With passengers, including on one occasion the Midland Railway's General Manager James Allport (Sir James from 1884), finding their 'express' attached to the back of slow-moving coal trains for the journey between Ingleton and Carlisle, it became clear that the Midland would have to do something to resolve the situation.

Serious negotiations between the two companies over better shared usage of the line came to nothing, and eventually the Midland determined to build its own dedicated route. Much earlier a Bill had been proposed by the North of England Union Railway for a line from a junction with the 'Little' North Western Railway at Settle to Hawes (originally to Kirkby Stephen, after which the plan was modified). This company soon found its plans superseded by those of another company – the Midland Railway! – and its original Bill was withdrawn and replaced by one for the entire route from Settle to Petteril Junction, Carlisle. This was the Settle to Carlisle route, authorised by Parliament by the Midland Railway (Settle & Carlisle) Act 1866. A considerable thawing of the relationship between the Midland and the LNWR Boards took place in 1868, and negotiations resumed on the possibility of allowing the MR joint access to the Lancaster & Carlisle line and improved access to Carlisle Citadel station, which had previously been the main bone of contention between the two companies. Flushed with success at the positive outcome of these resumed talks, the Midland now applied to Parliament for a Petition of Abandonment, feeling that the new line was no longer needed – but to no avail! Both the Lancashire & Yorkshire Railway (L&YR) and the North British Railway (NBR) had

Journey's end – or journey's beginning, depending on your direction of travel. A Leeds to Carlisle train sits at Carlisle Citadel, beneath reminders of the station's previous steam-days glory. *DJW*

been buoyed with enthusiasm over the expected new traffic that the Midland route would bring to their respective lines. In addition, the L&YR had an end in sight to its dependence on the LNWR at Preston, and the NBR, having invested heavily in its 'Waverley' route from Carlisle to Edinburgh, felt it was within touching distance of ending the 'second class' status of its trains at the hands of the LNWR at Carlisle. Parliament agreed with these arguments, and the Petition of Abandonment was refused; the Settle to Carlisle line would have to be built after all.

It was on 2 August 1875 that the line opened to goods traffic. It would be a further nine months, on Monday 1 May 1876, before the Settle & Carlisle opened to passenger trains. The bulk of the revenue was generated by freight traffic, in common with most other railway companies, though there were initially six daily London (St Pancras) to Carlisle Citadel services each way utilising the new route, consisting of two Scottish expresses, two semi-fast trains and two that called at all stations over the 'S&C'. The Midland could not compete with the LNWR on distance, as its route was longer and over more difficult terrain, but it could compete on fares and on comfort, using the recently introduced - Pullman Cars on its expresses between London and Glasgow.

Settle Junction station was an early closure in 1876, and though various signal boxes came and went, either replaced or taken out of commission, and the stations at Dent (1877) and Culgaith (1880) opened, the status quo largely prevailed during Midland Railway, and later London,

Midland & Scottish Railway (LMS) ownership. The branch to Hawes opened to goods on 1 August 1878 and to passengers on 1 October.

The S&C was heavily used during both the First and Second World Wars, although it was during the latter that the first of the intermediate stations closed. This was Scotby, the MR's most northerly station, which closed on 1 February 1942. The line passed to the Midland Region of British Railways upon nationalisation in 1948, and in the 1950s Crosby Garrett, Cotehill and Ormside stations (1952) and Cumwhinton (1956) succumbed.

The S&C route was not one scheduled for imminent closure in the Beeching Report of 1963, though its viability was seriously questioned; the report recommended withdrawal of passenger services, and goods facilities were to start being withdrawn. However, on 4 November 1964 the Government announced that it was to refuse, at least for the time being, the closure of the intermediate stations on the line and the consequent withdrawal of local services. With plans in hand to electrify the West Coast Main Line during the early 1970s, the S&C was seen as an important diversionary route while this work was being carried out. Even after electrification had been completed, some goods trains still had to use the S&C; there was a problem with slow freight trains intermingling with high-speed electric services on the main line, giving the diversionary route an added raison d'être.

A further reason was that 'unfitted' freight trains (which did not have operative brakes on all wagons in the consist) could not use a route that lacked catch points. Catch points were common on railways in the days before continuous automatic braking, and were a safety measure intended to derail wagons that had broken away from their train and were running away downhill, thus preventing them hitting a following train. The newly electrified West Coast Main Line had had this

Freight returned to the Settle & Carlisle line after a complete absence of four years in 1993-94, when Trainload Freight (succeeded by Transrail and latterly by English, Welsh & Scottish) won a 10-year contract to move desulphurised gypsum from Drax Power Station to the Kirkby Thore plasterboard factory. Here Class 60 No 60094 is pictured heading north at Blea Moor with the 04.46 Drax to Kirkby Thore working on 2 June 1997. *David Stacey*

safety feature removed, so unfitted trains naturally graduated to the Settle & Carlisle line. In due course, trains became air-braked throughout (as opposed to vacuum-braked), thus depriving the line of this additional advantage.

The Settle Junction to Appleby North Junction section closed to goods on 16 May 1983, then the Appleby North Junction to Petteril Bridge section closed to goods on 31 March 1989. This traffic would resume in 1993-94 with the start of gypsum trains from Drax, near Selby, to Kirkby Thore, north of Appleby between the former stations of Long Marton and New Biggin, both of which closed in 1970. However, before this, there would be many years of uncertainty over the line's very existence.

April 1966 saw the introduction of diesel multiple units (DMUs) to the route. The line was central to a poignant day in British railway history when, on 11 August 1968, crowds witnessed the last main-line workings of steam locomotives under the ownership of British Railways. The majority of stations, many of which had gradually been losing their goods facilities, closed to passenger traffic on 4 May 1970 – only Settle and Appleby remained open. This situation persisted for several years, but in the summer of 1975 a new initiative called 'Dales Rail' was introduced as a trial measure. The trains were sponsored by the Yorkshire Dales National Park Authority in partnership with Cumbria County Council, Eden District Council and the Countryside Commission, and saw British Rail carry out some basic renovation work at five stations (Horton-in-Ribblesdale, Ribblehead, Dent, Garsdale and Kirkby Stephen) in order to bring them up to a standard where passengers could use them on an occasional basis. The main aim of the trains was to give access to the National Park for those without their own transport, to act as a 'park and ride' alternative for those wishing to visit the National Park without driving into the area, and to provide local residents living along the line with a service that allowed them to make a day trip to either Carlisle to the north or West Yorkshire to the south.

Trains ran using DMUs as far as Appleby, where they terminated. The fact that over just 12 days of operation some 10,000 passengers were carried illustrated the line's passenger-carrying potential, and the following summer of 1976 saw services extended to three more northerly stations (Langwathby, Lazonby and Armathwaite) and running from more destinations. These services were to continue until the stations were reopened permanently in July 1986. Steam returned to the line on a trial basis during 1978, and this led to more steam workings gradually being introduced, most notably the 'Cumbrian Mountain Express', which was run from 1980 by the Steam Locomotive Operators Association (SLOA) in conjunction with British Rail, and later the 'Cumbrian Mountain Pullman'. Today steam specials (and occasionally diesel-hauled ones) are still a popular part of the Settle to Carlisle scene.

On one level this might have seemed wholly positive progress, yet it was counterbalanced by more disturbing developments in the early 1980s. Only three expresses between Nottingham and Glasgow still ran over the line, and British Rail announced that these would be permanently rerouted via Manchester and Preston. This occurred from 16 May 1982, and only two scheduled trains per day (Dales Rail specials excluded) were left to travel between Leeds and Carlisle, stopping only at Settle and Appleby on the S&C line. The remaining through freight traffic using the line was now diverted away, and the nightly parcels working was also sent by another route, allowing closure of the S&C between 10.00pm and 6.00am.

Against this backdrop the future of what is arguably the line's most famous structure, Ribblehead Viaduct, was called into question by a report quoting that a repair figure of up to £6 million would need to be spent within five years if the line was to remain open. On 17 November 1983 early notice of the intended cessation of passenger services came from British Rail. The intention was, essentially, to lift the lines at the south end of the line beyond Ribblehead, and at the northern end of the line below Appleby, taking out the centre section of the route entirely, saving on maintenance costs to Ribblehead Viaduct and leaving only the section of line in place over which freight was currently passing – from Ribblehead Quarry, and from Warcop via the junction with the former Eastern Region line at Appleby.

The closure proposals were met with fury and hostility, not only from local people but also from railway enthusiasts and supporters across the country. There was a widespread belief that British Rail had exaggerated the case for closure, not just in the civil engineering costs it estimated, but by quoting locomotive fuel and maintenance costs that might have got the Space Shuttle off the ground, let alone a diesel unit from Settle to Carlisle. The Friends of the Settle-Carlisle Line was formed on 27 June 1981 to fight the proposals, and this organisation joined with two others, the Railway

Freight workings today are predominantly hauled by Class 66 locomotives. Here, English, Welsh & Scottish's No 66059 heads south through Kirkby Stephen, the buildings of which have been rejuvenated by the work of the Settle & Carlisle Railway Trust. *DJW*

Development Society and Transport 2000, to form a coordinated response to the closure proposals under the banner of the Settle to Carlisle Railway Joint Action Committee. At the same time Cumbria County Council, supported by other local authorities and the tourist board, commissioned its own independent report into the line's future. A study was also commissioned by the Action Group, which recommended that a number of additional services might be viable along the route, both through and local. Sixteen days of hearings into the closure were held. A subsidy of more than £70,000 was forthcoming from local authorities at this time to sponsor extra trains under the title of 'Dalesman trains', so that extra regular services could run twice a day, calling at the stations only previously served by the weekend Dales Rail services; these started on 14 July 1986.

By the following year five trains each way per day were travelling over the line, passenger figures were soaring massively and profitability was increased. In March 1988 several local authorities agreed to put funds to the value of half a million pounds towards the repair of Ribblehead Viaduct, but by May of that year it was clear that the Conservative Government was intent on backing the closure proposals. After nearly a year of further wrangling, as the Government attempted to sell the line to private bidders and BR's scale of charges for using its tracks at each end of the Settle and Carlisle line in turn dashed each proposal, the then Secretary of State for Transport, Paul Channon, announced in a written answer to the House of Commons on 11 April 1989 that the line was to be reprieved, along with the associated Blackburn to Hellifield line, citing "changes in the financial case". Mr Channon believed that there was "scope for increasing revenue further by better marketing of the line and by the pricing of tourist journeys on a more commercial basis" and stated that, as required by statute, he had "also taken account of new evidence on hardship and the line's importance to the local economy".

Since then, a large amount of money has been invested in the infrastructure of the line, and organisations such as the Settle & Carlisle Railway Trust have taken over responsibility for and restored a number of buildings along the line. Freight usage of the line has grown remarkably, most notably through coal and gypsum traffic, but with additions such as the Blue Circle cement traffic from Hope in Derbyshire to Brunthill in Carlisle, and the line has on several occasions proved an invaluable asset as an alternative to the West Coast Main Line when the latter has been out of commission; electric units are diesel-hauled over the Settle to Carlisle route using Class 57 'Thunderbird' locomotives.

In the privatisation era passenger services were run by Arriva Trains Northern and First North Western. Today the passenger service is operated by Northern Rail, which was awarded the franchise on 1 July 2004 by the Strategic Rail Authority, its tenure commencing from 12 December of that year. Northern Rail is owned by Serco-NedRailways, which is a joint venture established in 2002 between the rail companies Serco, operators of the Docklands Light Railway, and NedRailways, whose parent company is NS Dutch Railways, which carries more than a million passengers each day in the Netherlands. The company has won both the titles Train Operator of the Year and Rail Business of the Year in recent times and has strived to make a difference to the communities it serves.

Although the line truly begins at Settle Junction and finishes at Petteril Junction on the approach to Carlisle, this book takes as its starting point Hellifield, and the end point as Carlisle Citadel station. This is because both of these stations are inextricably linked with the Settle to Carlisle story, and coverage would be incomplete without their inclusion. No conscious attempt has been made to draw a 'dividing line' on dates between 'past' and 'present'; the past has always gone, whether it was an hour ago or 100 years ago! While there are many decades of difference between some views, others are much closer together; for instance, Garsdale station in 2008 was significantly poorer than the beautifully refurbished station of 2009!

The line runs through countryside that is at times beautiful, at other times rugged, at other times spectacular. Despite the huge amount of prose written on the line, and the vast number of photographs taken of it, I have not yet seen an example of either that fully conveys its awe-inspiring nature, the breathtaking scenery through which it passes, the incredible engineering achievement that its building signifies, or the triumph over adversity that its continued presence represents.

The line, in common with the area through which it runs, has many moods; whether waiting in the doorway of a platform shelter on a windswept platform for a train to emerge from the mist, or lazily watching from your seat as the shadow of your train eases across the shadow of Ribblehead Viaduct traced out on the ground below on a warm and sunny summer evening, each evokes an element of the line's singular character. If this book succeeds in conveying just a fraction of the interest and atmosphere that surrounds this magnificent railway line, then it will have served a useful purpose.

David J. Williams
March 2010

Hellifield

The current Hellifield station was built by the Midland Railway and opened on 1 June 1880. Perhaps the most notable feature of the station is its cast-iron platform canopies, which, together with the station buildings, were restored in 1994 using a £500,000 grant from the Railway Heritage Trust and the local council, and have Grade II Listed status. There had been a North Western Railway station serving the town previously, which was opened in 1849 and located about a quarter of a mile south of the existing station. The Midland Railway station was located at the junction of the MR line from Leeds to Carlisle and the Lancashire & Yorkshire Railway's line from Blackburn, the station being built and paid for by the Midland and rented by the L&YR. The line from Blackburn lost its passenger traffic on 10 September 1962, and there was a gradual reduction in traffic calling at Hellifield, as local trains to Carlisle ceased calling from May 1970 and London to Glasgow expresses from 1975. These views looking towards the extensive shed show the station in 1912 (*above*) and in the 1960s; the contrast could not be more marked. Southbound trains travelling from Carlisle to Leeds call at this platform. *Both Lens of Sutton*

Although the scene above is clearly the same location as in the two pictures on the previous page, it would now be hard to imagine, if you didn't know, looking at the rusting tracks disappearing beneath burgeoning bushes and increasingly unrelenting undergrowth, that a vibrant motive power depot once existed here, closing in 1963. Extensive exchange sidings between the L&YR and MR were also located at Hellifield, and opened on 1 March 1880. The station was home to three signal boxes in its heyday, though only the South Junction box remains today. The station, at least, has received major investment and is now the home of The Long Drag Cafe, generally open seven days a week between 9.00am and 4.00pm for fireman's breakfasts, lunches and teas. Trains running from Leeds to Carlisle began to call again at Hellifield in May 1995, and today it is often the starting point for steam haulage on specials over the S&C. Below we have a glimpse of the depot in its heyday, on 2 October 1948, with 'Black Five' No 4909 and 4-4-0 No 4188 on shed. *DJW/H. C. Casserley*

Hellifield's locomotive depot had four roads, a turntable and a coaling stage. Midland 4-4-0s would have been regular performers over the S&C in Midland Railway days and here No 456, a '483' (or 'No 2') Class superheated 4-4-0, stands outside the shed on 30 June 1933. Dating from the 1890s, No 456 was rebuilt with a 'G7' boiler in March 1920 and survived into BR service, being withdrawn in November 1949. *H. C. Casserley*

Ex-Midland Railway 0-6-0 No 3137 stands on the shed on 12 June 1947. Originally No 1705 of the Johnson-designed '1698' Class, No 3137 entered traffic in March 1885. Though some other members of the class were designated Class 2, this was one of 11 Class 3 '1698' 0-6-0s to pass into British Railways service in 1948, becoming No 43750. It was withdrawn in November 1959, but the last surviving member of the class (LMS No 3185/BR No 43185) soldiered on until September 1961. *H. C. Casserley*

On 23 April 1954 former Lancashire & Yorkshire Railway 2-4-2T No 50686 is seen at Hellifield, while 2-6-4T No 42473 is on the turntable; whether a turntable will ever be reinstated here in connection with steam specials remains to be seen. In addition to the locomotives stabled at the shed, two snowploughs were also based here for use during the severe winter months. *Both H. C. Casserley*

Above: **This is the interior of Hellifield depot (23B) on 1 June 1963; it closed on the 17th, so is seen during its last few weeks of operation. Fowler 4F 0-6-0 No 44479, 2-6-4T No 47492 and 'Black Five' No 45602 are pictured, together with a rail-mounted crane.**

Following closure, the depot was used to store stock from the National Collection destined for Clapham Transport Museum. In the centre picture, nearest the camera is James Holden-designed 1905-built Great Eastern Railway 'G58' Class 0-6-0 No 1217E (carrying LNER livery, when it was reclassified as a 'J17'), while the third view shows LNWR Ramsbottom 0-4-0T No 1439.
H. C. Casserley/David J. Mitchell (2)

LMS 2-6-4T No 21 awaits departure from the south-end bay at Hellifield on 28 April 1949, possibly bound for Blackburn. Sixty years later, during May 2009, a Leeds-bound train calls at the main platform. As can be seen, the chances of a departure any time soon from the bay platform are remote! However, the station area and its buildings have huge potential for railway use, were substantial investment ever to become available.
H. C. Casserley/DJW

Today, freight trains requiring a path often wait in the southbound platform; here a Freightliner coal train is stopped waiting for the road. *DJW*

Below left: A detail from the restored Midland Railway canopy: this example incorporates the MR monogram, while elsewhere the Wyvern, the emblem of Mercia, can be seen, which was incorporated into the Midland Railway's coat of arms. The second picture, *below right,* is an interesting view showing how the Midland Railway set pillars in place in the platform. *Both DJW*

Opposite top: **Ex-Midland Railway 4-4-0 No 1142 waits to leave the bay platform at the north end of the station with the 11.45am service to Carlisle on 2 October 1948. The second view of the empty platform,** *above,* **is dated 1 June 1963. As can be seen from the 2009 view,** *below,* **the majority of the signalling has gone, as has the bay platform track, platform lighting and running-in boards.** *H. C. Casserley (2)/ DJW*

A northbound special waits to depart on 4 September 1955. Note that by that date the canopy had been shortened from its position in 1948, but that there has been little change to the extent of the structure from then until the present day. The views on this and the previous pages all reveal changes to the station lighting (as, technically, do the 2009 views!). *H. C. Casserley*

The 'present' view shows a northbound passenger train pulling out bound for Carlisle. *DJW*

Long Preston

Long Preston opened in July 1849 and is the first station to the north through which the line passes after leaving Hellifield en route to Settle Junction, where the Settle & Carlisle line diverges from the route to Morecambe. It originally had a Station Master's house, waiting room, booking office, goods yard with weighbridge, platelayers' hut and a gas works, though the latter had closed by 1917. The scale of the buildings in the early 1900s can be seen here, while the more modest provisions made for present-day passengers can be seen on the platforms in 2009. *Lens of Sutton/DJW*

The main buildings at Long Preston were demolished in January 1972. The signal box, also now demolished, can still be seen beyond the bridge in this early 1970s view, though the 'bus stop'-style waiting shelter has already appeared; note the two sets of portable steps to aid passengers boarding and alighting.

In the spring of 2009 Class 66 No 66509 passes through the station having traversed the Settle to Carlisle line to bring its coal wagons southwards. The station appears better cared for today than in the 1970s, with significantly more lighting provided for passengers and a well-maintained platform surface. *Lens of Sutton/DJW*

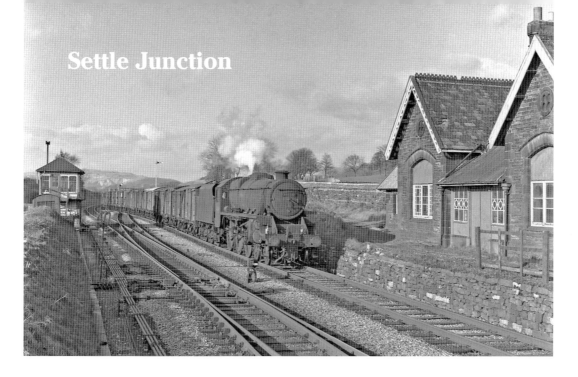

Settle Junction

Opened 1875, closed 1 November 1877 is not, perhaps, the most glowing of epitaphs to be attached to a station, though this is the dubious distinction accorded to Settle Junction. The town was served by two other stations, at Giggleswick (Settle old station) and the surviving Settle & Carlisle line station (Settle new), so maybe, taking into account the junction's isolated position, three was too much of a crowd. The station building was later converted into a ganger's cottage, and is seen here on the right of the picture as 'Black Five' 4-6-0 No 44854 passes with a southbound goods train in 1965; the building has since been demolished. *David J. Mitchell*

The different levels of the lines to Morecambe on the right and Settle on the left can be seen as British Railways 9F 2-10-0 No 92249 begins the climb. No 92249 was allocated new to Newport (Ebbw Junction) in December 1958 and moved to Carlisle Kingmoor in June 1964, where it remained until transfer to Speke Junction in January 1968; it was withdrawn in May 1968. *David J. Mitchell*

Contrasts in diesel motive power at Settle Junction: in March 1966 a Sulzer Type 4 'Peak' begins the climb, with the Morecambe line branching off in the foreground; the station building, which lasted until the late 1960s, is still standing.

Thirty years later, on 30 November 1996, Class 60 No 60038 in Loadhaul livery passes the same location with the 10.40 Drax to Kirkby Thore train. The trackwork at the junction was remodelled following the derailment of a northbound freight train on 1 May 1979, and the pointwork has been renewed at this location as recently as July 2009. The signal box, the third at this site, was operational from 14 September 1913, having replaced a box of 1892 vintage, which had itself been a replacement for the 1874 original. A second (south) signal box was located at Settle Junction until late 1922. *David J. Mitchell/David Stacey*

Settle

Settle station is pictured on 7 May 1965 and in September 2008. The addition of the footbridge is the most obvious change; it was formerly located at Guiseley, Leeds, but became redundant when the Wharfedale line on which Guiseley is situated was electrified, and was moved to Settle; once opened, the foot crossing at the end of the platform was closed. The Friends of the Settle-Carlisle Line have a shop here, raising valuable funds to help them in their work as a user group, promoting the route through leaflet production and distribution, coordinating volunteers to tend flowerbeds as part of the Station Adoption Scheme, and restoring features along the line, such as the signal boxes at Settle and Armathwaite. The Friends are involved in a number of other capacities along the line, including care of platform benches, providing on-train guides, manning the shops at Settle and Appleby, and liaising with many groups including Network Rail, Northern Rail and the Yorkshire Dales National Park Authority. A recent innovation has been working with BBC radio presenter Mark Holdstock and Northern Rail to produce an audio guide to the line, which can be downloaded from the internet as MP3 files, or can be purchased pre-loaded on MP3 players available from Settle station shop. The organisation has around 3,500 members and produces a quarterly magazine, and anyone interested in joining should visit www.settle-carlisle.org or pick up a leaflet at any of the stations along the route. *H. C. Casserley/DJW*

Settle Station signal box, closed in 1984, was relocated in 1997 by the Friends of the Settle-Carlisle Line to a new position away from the running lines at the south end of the platform; a fine display of signalling equipment has been restored and is demonstrated to visitors on days when the signal box is open. It won the Westinghouse Signalling Award for the Best Restored Signal Box or Signalling Installation at the 2008 National Railway Heritage Awards, jointly with the Llangollen Railway for the latter's restored signal box at Carrog. The award was presented by *Antiques Roadshow* expert Paul Atterbury at a ceremony at the Merchant Taylors' Hall in London in December 2008 and was unveiled in its new position in the signal box by entertainer Mike Harding on Wednesday 22 April 2009. Also in 2009, a new starter signal was erected for display outside the signal box. The former water tower is still in position behind what is now the station car park.

Pictured opposite in the restored signal box is Derek Soames. Derek worked for 50 years on the line, starting in 1945 as a porter at Settle station and moving into signalling after a period of National Service, retiring in 1995. He admits that he thoroughly enjoyed every minute of it. Derek remains an active volunteer with the Friends, and a steward on charter trains along the route. *All DJW*

The view of Settle on 7 May 1965 shows the watering facilities for northbound locomotives in the right foreground and the barrow crossing used by passengers prior to the erection of the footbridge in the 1990s. In the middle distance, the former location of the signal box, to the south of the station and directly in front of the goods shed, can be seen.

The second view shows the station buildings as they were in autumn 2008. Inset in two of three recesses in the brickwork are Mickey Mouse, who first appeared in 1963, and Minnie Mouse! *H. C. Casserley/DJW*

An engineering train passes through Settle in May 2009. The Station Master's house, now in private ownership, can be seen on the right. Between November 2008 and August 2009, Northern Rail refurbished the station, providing new toilets (including a new disabled toilet), new staff facilities for the Booking Office, replacement windows where necessary and repaired bargeboards. The ladies' toilet has been moved, meaning that the room previously designated a Ladies Waiting Room has now become a general passenger information room. Funding from North Yorkshire County Council enabled that area to be fitted out with a screen showing live running information, and the station has been fully repainted. In September 2009 Settle station gained the Station of the Year award in the Small Station category of the National Rail Awards; this award is given to stations that excel in providing a smooth, efficient and pleasant departure and arrival point for their travelling customers. Enterprise is not new to Settle, for in the 1960s the then Station Master Mr Jim Taylor persuaded British Rail to stop six expresses per day at the station and, as a consequence, ticket sales rose by 40% in just one year (1966). *DJW*

Accident near Settle station, 21 January 1960

At around 1.48am on 21 January 1961 British Railways Standard 7MT Class 'Pacific' No 70052 *Firth of Tay*, then based at Polmadie in Glasgow, was at the head of the 9.05pm express working from Glasgow (St Enoch) to London (St Pancras) when it was involved in a derailment around half a mile north of Settle station, between bridges 10 and 11.

As seems to be the case in many of the worst accidents to have occurred on the line, it happened in atrocious weather conditions in the middle of the night. The driver of the locomotive had been concerned by an unfamiliar 'knock' coming from 70052 earlier in the journey but, in poor weather, his inspection in the dark during a stop at Garsdale did not reveal that the locomotive's slide bar bolts had worked loose, causing two bottom right-hand slide bars to fall off. The first was lost some 30 miles prior to the accident site, with a second falling off 22 miles nearer. The driver decided to continue to Hellifield at reduced speed, where a more thorough inspection might be made. As the train was nearing Settle station, the loco's piston rod fractured and dug into the ballast to a depth of up to 6 feet, which in turn probably caused a misalignment of the adjoining track. (It should be noted that, due to the inclement weather and the need to reopen the line quickly, no accurate survey of the damaged track was carried out, so the exact cause of the derailment was not fully established.) A northbound goods train headed by 'Mogul' No 42881 passing in the opposite direction was also derailed, the loco and first eight vehicles coming off the line and ending up in such a position that it hit the carriages of No 70052's train. Many of the carriages of the express were badly damaged, with the first three vehicles having their sides almost completely torn open by the front of the goods locomotive, and five being badly scored with smashed windows and four doors being torn off. Five passengers were killed and eight more were injured, together with the guard of the goods train. The accident was attributed to poor maintenance, the loose slide bar bolts responsible on this occasion not being a unique occurrence for this class of locomotive, and having been reported on nine occasions previously on this locomotive alone; though tightened several times, these, and other related components, had never actually been replaced, though the official report did draw attention to the difficulty of maintenance on a relatively difficult-to-access part of the locomotive.

Helwith Bridge

Approaching Helwith Bridge are two 8Fs led by No 48321 with a train of concrete sleepers bound for Gretna, heading north in August 1967. Between 1926 and 1969 there was a siding here and an associated ground frame serving the Helwith Bridge Granite Company. Helwith Bridge also had an operational signal box between 21 August 1876 and 7 September 1969; the signal box and ground frame were taken out of use on the same day. Today, all material is moved from the quarries by road by a procession of heavy lorries.

Nearly 42 years later, in May 2009, First GBRf Class 66 No 66713 passes the same spot, with wagons bound for the Gypsum Works at Kirkby Thore. *David J. Mitchell/DJW*

Horton-in-Ribblesdale

On 25 August 1962 an 8F 2-8-0 heads a goods train south through Horton-in-Ribblesdale, then, firmly in the 'Corporate Blue' era, a four-car DMU calls at the station in May 1989 with a southbound train for Leeds. The inset shows the warm greeting extended today to visiting enthusiasts by local residents! *David J. Mitchell (2)/DJW*

The signal box at Horton-in-Ribblesdale from a northbound train is seen on 15 July 1967. The box was commissioned on 9 August 1896 and remained in use until 1 May 1984, although the station had lost its goods traffic facility from 2 February 1965. The cattle dock was adjacent to the signal box, and a weigh office was also provided. The station closed to passengers on 5 May 1970, reopening in 1986. *H. C. Casserley*

This is something of a curiosity in that a brand new set of steps with railings for aiding passengers boarding and alighting at the station, in white and maroon livery, has been provided. However, in early 2009 this remains chained to the station drainpipes while a 'veteran' British Rail version, still in Corporate Blue livery and apparently 'loaned' from Kirkby Stephen's south platform, has been pushed forward for use by passengers. If I'd made the new one, I don't think I would allow anyone to use it either! *DJW*

Horton-in-Ribblesdale station is seen again in the 1960s and 2009. The superbly tended gardens and well-kept appearance of the station saw it win 17 consecutive Best Kept Station Awards during the steam era. Though the distinctive station sign has been replaced, the new board is completely in keeping with the Midland-style environs of the station. *Lens of Sutton/DJW*

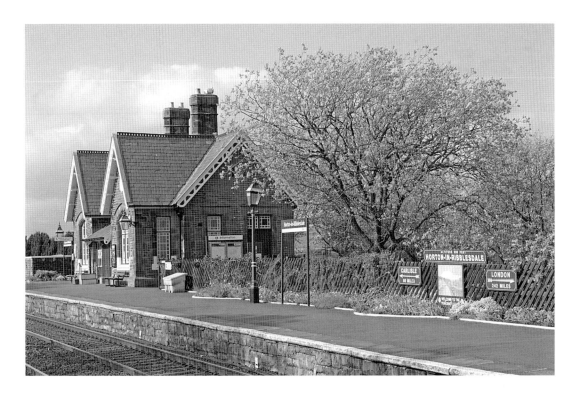

The station underwent refurbishment during 2003, during which time a small wooden waiting shelter was erected on the up platform. Funding was provided by the Settle & Carlisle Railway Trust, the Railway Heritage Trust, the Yorkshire Dales Millennium Trust, the National Park Authority, Friends of the Settle-Carlisle Line and Yorkshire Forward. From 14 November 2003 the building was leased for business use. These views show the station following restoration. *Both DJW*

Looking south from Horton-in-Ribblesdale station, with the signal box still in place, former Midland Railway 4F 0-6-0 No 43868 approaches with a northbound pick-up goods on 12 August 1953. The London, Midland & Scottish Railway continued to build what became classified as the '4F' 0-6-0s under the auspices of Sir Henry Fowler KBE (1870-1938), Chief Mechanical Engineer of the Midland Railway between 1925 and 1933, and all survived into British Railways ownership, the last examples being withdrawn in 1966; four have been preserved. This locomotive was introduced in 1918 and withdrawn in December 1960.

In May 2009 Class 66 No 66188 heads north with coal traffic. The trappings of the steam era railway are all now gone, with semaphore signals, the various sidings and telegraph poles all absent from the 'present' view. The Class 66s are easily the most numerous class of freight locomotive operating on Britain's rail network today and are the staple power for freight trains working over the Settle to Carlisle route. *D. Callum, Lens of Sutton/DJW*

A station was originally proposed for Selside, and though it never materialised four railway workers' cottages were (and still are) located here. Selside also had a four-lever signal box, opened on 16 June 1907 and closed on 30 November 1975, finding a new home in preservation at Carnforth. In 1967 a former Crosti-boilered 9F 2-10-0 slogs by with a goods. The Franco-Crosti boiler was first trialled on a 248-ton locomotive belonging to Belgium State Railways in 1932, the basic idea being that a feedwater heater acted as a secondary boiler, making the loco more efficient. Ten of these engines were built by British Railways in 1954, but did not produce the anticipated savings on fuel and were converted to the more standard design, though with a lower 8F power classification than their original 9F rating for the remainder of their careers.

A two-car service train passes the same spot in 2009; a coal train is just receding past the cottages. Note again the complete absence of telegraph poles and wires and signalling, which, in 1967, were a key part of the scene. *David J. Mitchell/DJW*

Ribblehead

Our journey now reaches Ribblehead, one of the most famous locations on the line. The station opened to passengers as Batty Green on 4 December 1876, with the first signal box to be located at this site opening around the same time. The originally proposed name for the station was Ingleton Road, and it was changed to Ribblehead from 1 May 1877. This is a well-known picture featuring two Midland Railway 2F 0-6-0s in the northbound platform at Ribblehead station on 28 December 1906, fitted with snowploughs and posed, one presumes, with the crew; a van is attached between the two locomotives. *Lens of Sutton*

The angled running-in board dates this as a pre-Second World War photograph, probably taken around 1900. Ribblehead station closed to goods traffic on 7 November 1966 and, in common with most other stations on the line, to passenger traffic from 4 May 1970. In the summer of 1975 this was one of the stations that was reopened at weekends to accommodate the Dales Rail services for ramblers, which began in that year. *Lens of Sutton*

Looking south at Ribblehead, 'Black Five' 4-6-0 No 44673 calls with the 3.35pm Bradford to Carlisle service on 30 May 1951. The picture is taken from the original down platform. Note the signal box located just beyond the end of the platform, which replaced the original structure of 1876; this 'new' box opened on 10 July 1898 and closed on 17 August 1969. Beyond lay the sidings of H. Austin. *H. C. Casserley*

In June 2009 a four-car formation led by No 158853 pulls away from the current down platform. Keen-eyed readers will have noted, above the south gable of the station in 1951, weather monitoring equipment in the shape of an anemometer. Ribblehead was a weather monitoring station in LMS and BR days from 1938 until 1970, the staff receiving special training to work the equipment, and sending out hourly reports. Restoring another of the line's traditions, the new electronic weather station was installed in 2004, funded by the Settle-Carlisle Railway Business Liaison Group to mark its reconstitution as the Settle-Carlisle Enterprise Network (SCENe), an organisation that promotes the well-being of the communities, economy and environment of the Settle & Carlisle corridor. New equipment to give the site a broadband connection was funded by the Friends of the Settle-Carlisle Line, and was operational from April 2009. *DJW*

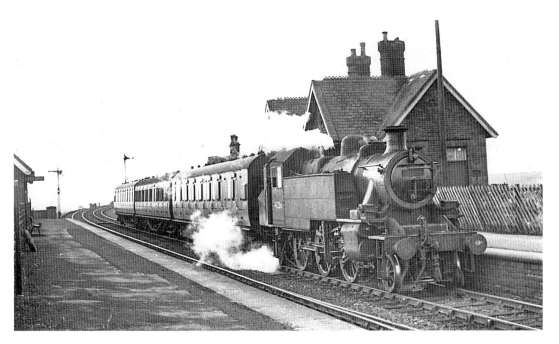

Ivatt 2MT 2-6-2T No 41206 arrives at Ribblehead station with 4.25pm from Hawes on 30 May 1951, and No 66613 heads a coal train past the same spot on 20 May 2009. The down platform from which the earlier picture was taken is no longer there, having been removed in 1974 to make way for the siding, the entrance to which can be seen to the left of the 'present' picture. The inset shows an advertisement for the 'Beauty Spot of the North', Ingleton, reached by turning left at the end of the station drive and keeping going! *H. C. Casserley/DJW*

The Settle & Carlisle Railway Trust

The new, staggered down (or northbound) platform at Ribblehead is seen here from the up platform, looking south. The funding of this structure was managed by the Settle & Carlisle Railway Trust, and this is, perhaps, an appropriate moment to take a brief look at the work of this organisation. *DJW*

The Trust is a Registered Charity. It was formed in 1990 with the primary objective of preserving, restoring and maintaining the historic structures and buildings along the line, and the secondary objective of promoting public knowledge and awareness of the line and the surrounding area. As mentioned above, an early project was managing the funding for the construction of the new platform at Ribblehead, together with that for the restoration of Ribblehead Viaduct. The Trust now owns the station buildings at Ribblehead,

and has negotiated a 125-year lease; restoration of what had become a heavily run-down station started in September 1999 and was completed in June 2000, earning the Trust the Ian Allan Heritage Award 2000. The Trust has also purchased the former Station Master's house at Ribblehead, the £150,000 purchase price being jointly and equally funded by the Trust and the Friends of the Settle-Carlisle Line. The project commenced in July 2006, and when a full restoration has been completed the building will be made available to let as holiday accommodation, and to host meetings and residential seminars.

The Trust's work is not restricted to Ribblehead alone, as the station buildings have been acquired at both Kirkby Stephen and Horton-in-Ribblesdale stations. The original Midland Railway station clock at Appleby has been restored, and five other stations on the route have been furnished with replica Midland clocks to add to the heritage ambiance of the line, courtesy of a number of generous donors and with the help of Martin Firth, who was responsible for the design, production and installation of the clocks.

Left: **In the first of these two views of Ribblehead station looking south, an unidentified 'Black Five' 4-6-0 arrives with a goods on the bitterly cold winter's day of 5 January 1963, while in May 2008 Freightliner Class 66 No 66511 heads north through the station. Taken from almost exactly the same position, the 1963 shot shows the down platform still in situ, with the signal box visible behind the tender and first two wagons of the train. In the background is the works of H. Austin, now demolished, and there is a crossover into the siding directly to the south of the platform; the fence marks the spot where passengers now cross the line to reach the newly built northbound platform. Power lines and their posts remain problematical for photography – some things never change!** *David J. Mitchell/DJW*

Following the derailment of a coal train near Dent Head in 1998, the subsequent 'clear-up' operation unearthed a set of wheels *(pictured below)* **from one of the contractor's wagons used in the construction of the line. The wheels were duly rescued, donated to the Settle & Carlisle Railway Trust by Railtrack and moved to Ribblehead station for display in September 2001, a move facilitated by the late Dr Robin Goodman.** *DJW*

Out and about

A Visitor Centre has been established at Ribblehead by the Settle & Carlisle Railway Trust. The facility is open from 9.30am to 4.30pm on Tuesdays to Sundays from March to October inclusive, and on Bank Holiday Mondays. During the winter months from November to February inclusive opening times are 9.30am to 4.30pm on Saturdays, Sundays and during school holidays only. Please note that these times may be subject to revision.

Adjacent to Ribblehead station is a quarry that yielded high-quality limestone for use in the iron industry in Durham. Activity began in 1943 and continued into the 1970s, with a powdering plant being built on the site to produce lime. The quarry then became dormant and in 1998 it was decided that further quarrying would destroy important stretches of limestone pavement, and the site's owner, Hanson Aggregates, agreed to give up its mineral extraction rights. After carrying out some landscaping work, Hanson handed over ownership of the site to English Nature in 2000, and the quarry is being allowed to return to its natural state, as birds and plants gradually recolonise the bare ground.

Free guided walks are organised by the Friends of the Settle-Carlisle Line to encourage use of Northern Rail's passenger services, both on the S&C and

Left: **On the approach to Ribblehead station from the north, 'Big Goods' (later 4F) 0-6-0 No 43999 is seen** *(inset)* **with a southbound goods on 30 May 1951. No 3999 was originally based at Toton and was one of ten members of the class (Nos 3997-4006) transferred to join the Durran Hill allocation in 1921, where it remained for several years; it was one of 22 to survive into 1965, being withdrawn in May of that year.**

In 2009 a gypsum train from Kirkby Thore, hauled by English, Welsh & Scottish Class 66 No 66187, rolls towards the station. The view is no less rich in scenery, but is decidedly lacking in signalling interest compared with the earlier picture. The transport of desulphogypsum (DSG) between Drax Power Station and Kirkby Thore by what was then Trainload Freight (TLF) in 1993-94 marked the return of freight traffic to the S&C route. *H. C. Casserley/ DJW*

on the Leeds to Lancaster and Morecambe line. Walks are graded in four categories of difficulty, and walk leaders meet participants as they leave trains at the station nearest to their starting point. These include tours of the area around Ribblehead Viaduct, when walkers can have the history of the site explained to them and can examine what is left of the archaeology on the site, which once accommodated the shanty towns for workers building the viaduct and Blea Moor Tunnel. Ribblehead tours, which last around 2 hours, usually run twice a day on Wednesdays in July and August, and details can be found on leaflets available at stations along the route.

Another organisation that promotes guided walks in the area from locations on the line is the Friends of Dales Rail. This group was formed in 1980 to support the Dales Rail services, detailed elsewhere, and promotes walks of easy, moderate and strenuous difficulty led by experienced walkers. More details can be obtained by calling 0113 293 1924 or by visiting the website at *www.friendsof dalesrail.org*.

Ribblehead Viaduct

Ribblehead (or Batty Moss) Viaduct is perhaps the most famous structure on the line. It has 24 arches (though 18 were originally considered) and rises to 105 feet above ground level at its highest point. A 1981 report gave the viaduct (and consequently the line as a whole) a life expectancy of around five years before closure if significant repairs were not carried out. British Rail was reluctant to spend the money, and began to divert traffic away from the S&C, which by now had only two stations, Settle and Appleby, open to passengers. Water damage from heavy and prolonged rainfall had eroded the mortar of the viaduct over the years, and the structure was deteriorating.

Once the campaign to save the line had ultimately proved successful, one of the priorities for funding was the repair of the viaduct. After lengthy initial examination in 1988 established the cost of repair – which was significantly less than the £4.25 to £6 million previously anticipated – 1989 saw plans for the first major phase of renovation put into action. The line was completely closed for two weeks during October 1989 and, working round the clock using electric lighting by night, significant renovation work was undertaken. The rails were lifted and the ballast removed, the latter being dumped over the side of the viaduct! Faults were repaired and the 'deck' of the viaduct was given a waterproof membrane. The parapet walls were strengthened with

concrete, then new ballast laid before the track was replaced. The line reopened on Monday 30 October 1989, with this most iconic structure given a new lease of life. In the photograph a service train is dwarfed by the structure in what is perhaps the most widely taken view of the viaduct, from the Ingleton road, looking towards Whernside. *DJW*

Two further phases of restoration took place, the final stage being completed during 1991, when a monument dedicated to the memory of the workers who built, maintained and restored the structure over the years was unveiled. It was subsequently refurbished and rededicated by Network Rail and the Friends of the Settle-Carlisle Line in 2005. *DJW*

A Stanier 'Jubilee' Class 4-6-0 crosses Ribblehead Viaduct with the down relief 'Thames-Clyde Express' in 1967, with the up 'Waverley' just visible at the south end of the viaduct. The 'Waverley' was the former 'Thames-Forth Express', which ceased running in 1939 and was not restored until 1957, when it carried the new title. While the 'Thames-Clyde Express' ran between London (St Pancras) and Glasgow, the 'Thames-Forth Express' ran between St Pancras and Edinburgh Waverley. The 'Waverley' ceased to run during the winter months as early as 1964, but continued to run during the summer until September 1968. *David J. Mitchell*

Building Ribblehead Viaduct

The first stone of Ribblehead Viaduct was laid by the contractor William H. Ashwell on 12 October 1870; he was the second contractor to work on the project, the first, John Ashwell, having encountered financial difficulties. William Ashwell was the Midland Railway's chosen replacement. Several shanty towns were established near the construction sites at Ribblehead and Blea Moor. These were named Jericho, Sebastopol, Salt Lake, Batty Green, Inkerman, Belgravia, Jerusalem, Tunnel Huts and Blea Moor, and housed the workmen who were engaged on the contract, together with their families. Some of the names came from victories in the Crimean War, others from the Bible; presumably Belgravia, after the upper-class area of London, was named with tongue firmly

Looking south towards Ribblehead station and Settle beyond in 1962, some temporary maintenance work is already being undertaken, six years before the end of steam, as a Class 5 4-6-0 with a down passenger train crosses the viaduct.

On a glorious spring day in May 2009 a service train crosses the viaduct. During the late 1970s and the very early 1980s the line across Ribblehead Viaduct was temporarily singled on a number of occasions, the first instance being from 1 October 1978. This also happened subsequently for periods during 1979 and 1980. Eventually the track across the viaduct was permanently singled, as from 13 January 1985, and is the only section of the line that is single-track. Behind is Penyghent (loosely translated as 'Hill of the Winds'); it is 694 metres (2278 feet) high, and together with Whernside (736m) and Ingleborough (723m) makes up the 'Three Peaks', which present such an exciting challenge to walkers.

The inset shows the nameplate *Ribblehead Viaduct*, which is on display at Settle station; this was the third name carried by Brush Type 4 No D1617 (later Class 40 Nos 47036, 47562 and 47760), its former names being *Sir William Burrell* and *Restless*. *R. Hewitt, Stephenson Locomotive Society/DJW*

in cheek. Wages were comparatively high for the time, but conditions relatively poor. In 1871 a smallpox outbreak saw the establishment of a smallpox hospital at Batty Green, including an oven, used to bake the clothes of infected patients. Contractors funded a school on site, which at one time had 43 pupils.

Bricks to line the tunnel and for the arches of the viaduct were manufactured on site at the Sebastopol Brickworks. The black limestone used in the construction of the viaduct was quarried from the bed of the stream in Littledale, the water's course being diverted by means of a small aqueduct.

A number of tramways were built to facilitate transport of materials around the Ribblehead site, as well as one from Batty Moss to the site of construction of Blea Moor Tunnel. A locomotive depot with an inspection pit, the site of which can still be seen, was located near the brickworks; it may have been covered by a wooden shed, though this is not certain. At least one contractor's locomotive was brought from the station at Ingleton to the Ribblehead site by road, towed by horses. Given the nature of the terrain and the comparatively poor state of local roads at the time, this must have been a considerable feat.

The viaduct and, of course, the rest of the line was designed by John Sydney Crossley (1812-1879). Crossley's railway career began on the Leicester & Swannington Railway in 1833. He later moved to the Midland Counties Railway, one of the three constituent companies of the Midland, and progressed to become Chief Engineer for the Midland Railway in 1858. He postponed his retirement to oversee construction of the Settle to Carlisle route, but resigned his position for health reasons in 1875 following completion of the line, remaining as a consultant.

Blea Moor

Steam at Blea Moor: 'Black Five' 4-6-0 No 44852 approaches Ribblehead Viaduct with a goods working on an unrecorded date, but firmly in the British Railways steam era, while nearer Blea Moor signal box another 'Black Five' heads a southbound passenger working towards Ribblehead. *Both R. Hewitt, Stephenson Locomotive Society*

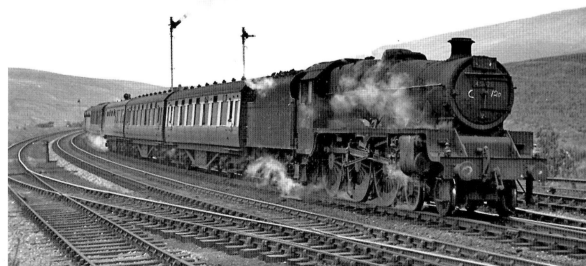

8F No 48074 heads north past Blea Moor on 4 November 1967, while a Fowler 4F 0-6-0 is seen in the up loop at the head of a pick-up goods in this panoramic view taken around 1956. *David J. Mitchell/R. Hewitt, Stephenson Locomotive Society*

A signal box originally opened at Blea Moor when the line opened to goods traffic on 2 August 1875. This was replaced on 4 December 1892, again on 28 June 1914 and once more on 16 December 1941. Also in 1941 the up lie-by siding was made into an up goods loop and the down No 1 lie-by siding was made into a down goods loop. The latter was decommissioned on 13 January 1985 when the track across Ribblehead Viaduct was permanently singled. The current signal box was renovated during the winter of 2002-03, with work including replacement double glazing and attention to the rotting woodwork of the operating cabin. At times, being rostered at Blea Moor appears to represent the signalling equivalent of solitary confinement, though in years gone by, when slower goods trains were frequently laid over here to allow faster expresses to pass, it was, by many accounts, quite a busy location. The southern entrance to Blea Moor Tunnel can be glimpsed in the middle distance beyond the overbridge in the 'present view'; to build the tunnel, at one mile 869 yards the longest on the line, men laboured for 12-hour shifts with only candles as illumination. The 'past' picture dates from 1970. *Kidderminster Railway Museum/DJW*

Sulzer Type 4 'Peak' No D14 heads northwards past Blea Moor box with the down 'Waverley' on 27 September 1963. Later to become Class 45 No 45015, this locomotive has been preserved and is now awaiting restoration at The Battlefield Line in Leicestershire. Note the water tower that once dominated the signal box. *H. C. Casserley*

In September 2009 a Class 158 unit passes the same location, now a touch overgrown. Staff accommodation in the form of two cottages and a house was provided here; the house survives, though the cottages do not. *DJW*

Dent Head and Arten Gill

The 10-arch Dent Head Viaduct stands 100 feet high and is 199 yards long; it was constructed between 1870 and 1875. A Class 47 heads across Dent Head Viaduct on 15 May 1982 with a southbound Glasgow to Nottingham working, while in May 2009 a Freightliner Class 66 and coal train are seen at the same location. *David J. Mitchell/DJW*

Beyond Dent Head to the north is another impressive structure, the curving 11-arch Arten Gill Viaduct, standing 117 feet tall and 220 yards in length. These views 'ancient and modern' provide two different perspectives of the viaduct. In the first, Stanier 'Black Five' 4-6-0 No 44722 heads south with a passenger working on 30 May 1951. In May 2009, seen from the footpath leading up from Cowgill, a Freightliner Class 66 rumbles over the viaduct with a coal train. *H. C. Casserley/DJW*

Dent

Crosti-boilered 9F 2-10-0 No 92021 approaches Dent station with a northbound goods working in 1967. By this time the station had lost its goods facilities, having been withdrawn from 1 October 1964. The solitary goods siding serving the yard at the south end of the station is already becoming overgrown after three years of disuse, though it was occasionally used for engineering work for some time. The signal box opened on 9 August 1891 and closed on 28 January 1981.

The Station Master's house, which was an early example of a double-glazed building due to its exposed location, is seen in the background just above the signal box. Following closure, the station building was used first as a school, then as an Outward Bound Centre, but still in the ownership of British Rail. After privatisation Dent station passed from British Railways ownership to Railtrack, which sold the station into private ownership in 1985, when it was purchased by Neil Ambrose. Over the course of the next 20 years Mr Ambrose restored the station, and in 2006 it was purchased by quantity surveyor Robin Hughes. Mr Hughes undertook more work and further upgraded the property, turning it into self-catering holiday accommodation. Today the station is privately owned and has been totally refurbished for use as fully furnished holiday accommodation with three bedrooms and full central heating. The former waiting room is now the lounge, though it retains the original fireplace, while the former ladies waiting room has now become the kitchen. One of the bedrooms is in the former porter's room, and another was originally the ticket office. More details can be obtained by visiting www.dentstation.co.uk. This is the highest main-line station in England, at 1,150 feet above sea level. *David J. Mitchell*

Dent station is seen in 1912 and in August 2008. In the 'present' picture preserved British Railways 7MT 4-6-2 No 70013 *Oliver Cromwell* passes through northbound at the head of a special railtour. The 'Britannias' were familiar locos over the Settle to Carlisle route in the later days of steam, No 70013 being one of the last steam locos over the route in August 1968. The fencing on the hillside was designed to try and prevent snow from drifting onto the line during harsh northern winters, of which there were many. *Lens of Sutton/DJW*

Dent station opened to goods and passenger traffic from 6 August 1877, and was located at Cowgill (earlier referred to as Monkeybeck), some 4 miles from the village of Dent and part-way up a narrow road with a gradient of 1 in 4, which can still be treacherous in winter weather; this road was (and sometimes still is) known as the 'Coal Road', and leads eventually to Garsdale across wild and beautiful terrain. Two alternative sites are believed to have been actively considered for the station, the others being at Arten Gill and Dent Head, though these would have been 7 or 8 miles from the village, nearly double the distance that passengers had to travel to use the eventually chosen site.

On 26 January 1963 Stanier 'Black Five' 4-6-0 No 45737 passes north through the station with a goods working, while in May 1989 double-headed Class 31s pass the same location with a special working. *Both David J. Mitchell*

This is the view looking north towards Garsdale and Carlisle on 30 May 1951. The waiting room on the up platform has been set into the hillside, presumably as additional weather protection. The station lost its passenger facilities on 4 May 1970, reopening from 29 September 1986. *H. C. Casserley*

It is seen again in September 2008. There is a new waiting shelter on the northbound platform to cater for passengers who would formerly have used the station building; this opened on 5 April 2001. Three brand-new shelters on the route have been provided by the Settle-Carlisle Railway Development Company, a not-for-profit partnership formed in 1992 to fund some of the infrastructure projects along the line, and instrumental in expanding ticket-selling activities at Appleby and Settle stations. The Development Company promotes both the S&C route and the line between Leeds, Lancaster and Morecambe. *DJW*

Contrasting forms of motive power arrive at Dent with southbound workings. During the 1960s Stanier 'Black Five' No 44672 arrives with an up express, while in May 2009 Class 66 No 66161 hauls the daily gypsum train; the latter working was several hours late, due to the failure of a coal train near Ribblehead earlier in the day. Note that the white-painted square on the bridge that acted as a 'sighting board' is still in evidence today, many years after the signal (itself painted black and white as a further aid to visibility) has been removed. *R. Hewitt, Stephenson Locomotive Society/DJW*

There are few really noticeable changes at Dent in the years between these two photographs, the first taken during the 1960s, and the more recent view dating from 2009. The fencing is much the same, though as the station is now in private ownership the building is fenced off from the platform. The main station building is now Grade II Listed. In 2008 the model railway company Hornby announced that it was to release a station building in its OO scale Skaledale range of lineside buildings based on Dent station, named Skaledale East. The bridge carries what is known as the 'Coal Road' over the railway as it winds its way to Garsdale; it is thought to have gained its name from the small drift mines that were opened on the fells, following the discovery of a coal seam in the middle of Rise Hill Tunnel, between Dent and Garsdale, while the line was being built! *Lens of Sutton/DJW*

To the right of the signal box in this 30 May 1951 view looking south along the platform can be seen the 'snow hut', a structure dating from 1885 that was built to give shelter to railway employees in this isolated location, whether working on the track or, in severe winter weather, helping to retrieve stranded trains from snow drifts. *H. C. Casserley*

Today the signal box, sidings and associated semaphore signalling are only memories, and the 'snow hut' has been restored and refurbished as accommodation that can be rented for self-catering holidays, with a double bedroom, bathroom, kitchen and, perhaps most importantly given the location, underfloor heating! The 'present' picture, taken in 2008, shows the Midland-style platform lights just coming on as dusk approaches. *DJW*

Heading north from Dent, the line passes through Rise Hill Tunnel (formerly known as Black Moss Tunnel), 1,213 yards long and built between 1870 and 1875. The Rise Hill site, home to one of the many settlements of navvies that sprung up during the building of the line, featured in an episode of Channel 4's *Time Team* archaeological programme, first broadcast on 1 February 2009.

Beyond, near milepost 256, is the site of the former Garsdale water troughs, designed to allow steam locomotives to take water while 'on the move' using a scoop in the tender. The water was chemically treated before entering the troughs to prevent corrosion occurring in the locomotive's boiler. The water trough was among the inventions of the engineer John Ramsbottom (1814-1897), who was Locomotive Superintendent of the Manchester & Birmingham Railway; this later became part of the LNWR, and Ramsbottom became District Superintendent for the North Eastern Division, and later Locomotive Superintendent of the Northern Division. After retiring from the LNWR, he became a Director of both the Lancashire & Yorkshire Railway, for whom he was a consulting engineer, and the Manchester-based locomotive builder Beyer Peacock. The first water troughs were installed by the LNWR at Mochdre on its Chester to Holyhead route around 1860.

Heading north over Garsdale troughs on 30 May 1951 is 4-6-0 No 46103 (still with LMS on its tender, some three years after nationalisation) in charge of a passenger express, while leaving Garsdale on the same day and heading towards Dent, 8F 2-8-0 No 48401 has reached the 1,670-feet-long troughs. As may be deduced from the latter photograph, taking water at the troughs could be an 'interesting' experience for those travelling near the front of passenger trains if the carriage windows were open! Garsdale troughs were the highest in Britain, their water tower, at one time steam-heated to guard against freezing winter weather, coming into use on 22 October 1907, and remaining operational until March 1968. *Both H. C. Casserley*

Garsdale

Garsdale station, at 1,130 feet above sea level, opened on 1 August 1876 and was originally known as Hawes Junction station, being the junction for the branch line to Hawes, where the Midland connected with the North Eastern Railway. In January 1900 the station was renamed Hawes Junction & Garsdale, and became known simply as Garsdale from September 1932. Goods facilities were withdrawn on 6 April 1964, though track and signalling associated with the goods yard and the Hawes branch, the Midland section of which closed in March 1959, remained in situ until January of the following year. The station closed to passengers on 5 May 1970 and reopened on 16 July 1986. On 30 May 1951 former LNER 'D20' Class 4-4-0 No 62391, with the 4.23pm mixed train from Northallerton, arrives in the branch platform.

In the second view, dating from 26 April 1954, we see a train from Hawes in the branch platform in a view looking south towards Settle. In the left background is the water tank and tank house, the bottom portion of which was used as a village hall after the First World War. A coach body was also located next to the water tank to act as a refreshment room during local dances. The tank house was demolished in 1971. The MR originally planned to locate a large shed here, on a scale comparable with that proposed for Carlisle, with stabling facilities for some 24 locomotives, but what transpired was a more modest structure on the up side of the line beyond the south end of the station; it was rented by the North Eastern Railway and later the LNER, and was used for shedding and servicing NER locos working the Hawes branch. It closed in 1939, having previously been rebuilt following a fire in early October 1917, seriously damaging a tank locomotive residing within. *Both H. C. Casserley*

Looking north towards Carlisle on 26 April 1954 No 45013 sits in the branch platform, while in the 'present' view we see the station in June 2009. Though the path of the branch tracks can be clearly seen, today its function is to accommodate the occasional car. The water columns and semaphore signals (that in the foreground dating from 1942), together with many other trappings of the steam era, have obviously long since been removed. However, the buildings on the down platform remain structurally the same, though now in pristine condition. The water tower behind the down platform (*inset*) is still in situ, though now employed in a more domestic setting. *H. C. Casserley/DJW (2)*

This is the approach to Garsdale station from the north, with Dandry Mire Viaduct in the left background. Ivatt 2MT 2-6-2T No 41206 arrives with the 4.25pm branch train from Hawes on 30 May 1951.

On 20 May 2009 Freightliner Class 66 No 66527 passes through on the main line with a southbound coal working. The tracks on which No 41206 ran in 1951 were lifted in January 1965, the back platform being taken out of use on the 17th of that month. The turntable (see page 67) was located in the middle distance between the signal post and the viaduct. *H. C. Casserley/DJW*

Ex-Midland Railway '1798' Class 0-6-0 No 3731 approaches Garsdale on the main line on 7 June 1938 with a short goods working. Designed by Johnson and built by Neilson in 1901, No 3731 (originally No 2702) had already undergone two rebuildings by the time of this photograph, as an 'H' Class in 1908 and a 'G7' Class in 1923. The loco became BR No 43731 and would not be withdrawn until July 1959. *H. C. Casserley*

A pair of Class 158 units led by No 158795 passes the same spot in September 2008. The path of the Hawes branch and associated sidings can still be seen today, to the right of the picture. *DJW*

The famous turntable at Garsdale is seen on 26 April 1951. The pit where the turntable was located can still be seen on the west (down) side of the line, to the left of the track from northbound trains, the right from southbound trains, between the station and Dandry Mire Viaduct.

As the Midland Railway operated a 'small engine' policy for many years, it was necessary to provide pilot or banking locomotives over the steeper parts of the route. These additional locos would be detached at Ais Gill and would then return to Garsdale for turning prior to returning to their home sheds. One evening the turntable was caught by a merciless wind and continued to spin, together with a locomotive, until platelayers filled in the turntable pit with earth and sand to halt its progress. This incident later featured as a story in one of the Rev W. Awdry's famous 'Thomas the Tank Engine' books, and resulted in the stockade seen here being built to shield locomotives from the worst ravages of the wind when being turned.

The turntable itself was removed in 1990 and is now located in operational condition at Keighley station on the Keighley & Worth Valley Railway, where it is seen in May 2000 with visiting Furness Railway No 20 in the process of being turned. *H. C. Casserley/ DJW*

'Black Five' 4-6-0 No 45013 with a 'minimalist' goods train heads towards the station past the turntable. *H. C. Casserley*

Accident near Garsdale (Hawes Junction), 24 December 1910

The line immediately to the north of Garsdale (then Hawes Junction) was the scene of a major accident in the early hours of 24 December 1910. This was a night of heavy traffic and even heavier rain, and by 5.00am some nine pilot locomotives from various trains, six 4-4-0s and three 2-4-0s, had amassed at the station and were waiting to be returned to their depots of Leeds or Hellifield to the south and Carlisle Durran Hill to the north. Two Class '2' 4-4-0s, Nos 448 and 548, had been turned ready to return north to Carlisle and, coupled together, were waiting at the down main starting signal. The signalman sent 2-4-0s Nos 247 and 249 south to Leeds coupled together, then accepted the down sleeping car express, the midnight working out of St Pancras, from Dent signal box to the south. The express was duly accepted by the Ais Gill signalman to the north of Garsdale, and the Garsdale signalman duly lowered the down main starting signal, having forgotten that the two light engines were already waiting to proceed to Carlisle. As the signal dropped the locos, whose crew had not reminded the signalman of their presence, moved off towards Ais Gill; though they whistled, the sound was obviously lost amidst the terrible weather and the sound of so many other locos being prepared around the station. Three minutes later, with the signal still 'off', the down express, headed by 4-4-0 No 549, piloted by 2-4-0 No 48, raced through the station on its way to Carlisle and Scotland; it never completed its journey.

The express caught the preceding locos, which were travelling sedately at less than half the speed of the train bearing down on them, immediately to the north of Lunds Viaduct, between Garsdale and Ais Gill Summit. Twelve passengers died in the crash and ensuing inferno, caused by oil-compressed gas leaking from the carriages and setting the train alight, though amazingly all eight members of the footplate crews escaped with their lives.

The Midland Railway Traffic Committee had approved the use of the Pintsch system of lighting for the carriages of its Scottish expresses, a method that utilised compressed oil gas, at its meeting of 19 March 1885, and this had been in use ever since. The system was invented by the German manufacturer Carl Friedrich Julius Pintsch (1815-1884) and used compressed gas derived from distilled naphtha, a flammable liquid mixture of hydrocarbons. The gas in the lamps that used the Pintsch system burned brighter and longer than the oil lamps that preceded it, and could withstand the vibration of a moving train without being extinguished. These considerations, together with its cost-effectiveness, seem to have been a major factor in the system being favoured, though it undoubtedly worsened the effect of an already tragic accident. Pintsch gas was later used successfully in unmanned lighthouses and beacons.

Following the accident, the Midland Railway determined to provide tools, rescue equipment and fire extinguishers on the stock used for long-distance journeys, both on its own dedicated trains and on joint services. Two new sleeping cars ordered in January 1911 to replace those destroyed in the accident near Garsdale were equipped with the Stone electric lighting system, though Pintsch gas continued to be used on existing cars; this would again have devastating consequences when a further accident occurred on the same stretch of line less than three years later.

The first of these two views looking south towards Settle was taken in 1954, the second in 2009. The signalling has been heavily rationalised and the water tank and tank house are now things of the past, though the signal box and fencing are largely the same. Note the different style of chimney evident on the up platform following restoration, the addition of traditional-style heritage lighting and the appearance of Ruswarp on his plinth in the centre of the flower bed on the extreme left (see page 71). Between 1892 and 1909 two signal boxes served the station, both on the down side of the line, beyond the north and south ends of the platform; in 1909 the facilities were combined in the present box on the down platform, which opened on 10 July 1910 and operated until 1983, its last day of use being 17 November 1983 as an emergency measure to allow West Coast Main Line traffic to be diverted over the S&C, though it had ceased to be used regularly several months earlier. It is now in full use again. *H. C. Casserley/DJW*

This somewhat more recent 'past and present' comparison shows the station under renovation during the 2008 season and after completion in 2009. The last previous major rebuilding work on the waiting room and booking office had taken place in 1957. The major restoration and upgrading work, carried out by Network Rail, started on 15 July 2008, and included provision of modern toilet facilities, heating and lighting and much repair to the internal and external structures on the station. Investment such as this would have been unthinkable when the line was at its most threatened in the 1980s, and is an indication of the healthy state of the line and the renewed commitment to maintaining the route for both freight and passenger use. In July 2009 the station was highly commended in the Network Rail Partnership Awards, alongside the Forth Bridge and the rail bridge at York Holgate; from a total of more than 350 entries, these were surpassed only by Newcastle's High Level Bridge, strengthening work on which won the competition. *Both DJW*

These two 2009 views, *(above and below left),* shows the excellent restoration work carried out on the interior of the down platform waiting room at Garsdale, with fireplace, seating, lighting, heating, new information boards by professional designer Pam Harrington, telephone and a small tourist information point. *Both DJW*

One of the new landmarks at Garsdale is a bronze statue to Ruswarp, *(below right),* a border collie and valid objector to the closure of the line back in the 1980s, being a fare-paying passenger who would suffer hardship should the line close. Ruswarp was the canine companion of Graham Nuttall who, together with David Burton, was one of the founder members of the Friends of the Settle-Carlisle Line. Graham died while out walking in the Welsh mountains at the age of just 41, disappearing on 20 January 1990. His body was found 11 weeks later, together with Ruswarp, who had refused to leave his master's side even in death; he was rescued and nursed back to health, living just long enough to attend Graham's funeral.

A letter in a newspaper suggested that a statue should be commissioned to commemorate Graham Nuttall and Ruswarp and, in due course, the Friends of the Settle-Carlisle Line launched an appeal. The statue was sculpted by Joel Walker and was unveiled on 11 April 2009 by Mrs Olive Clarke OBE DL, former chairman of the public hearings for the North West into the line's proposed closure, and Mr Ron Cotton, the former British Rail senior manager who, ironically, had been given the job of closing the line back in the 1980s. *DJW*

Hawes

The Midland Railway's Hawes branch was effectively the fifth contract in the building of the Settle to Carlisle line. The station at Hawes, operated jointly with the North Eastern Railway, was authorised by the Midland Railway (Settle & Carlisle) Act 1866 and the North Eastern Railway (Leyburn and Hawes Etc) Act 1870. Both the MR and the NER referred to their respective routes into Hawes as 'the Hawes branch'; the former held running powers for all traffic over the NER line between Hawes and Leyburn, while the NER had running powers for all traffic between Hawes Joint station and Settle Junction. However, there is no evidence that the Midland (and later the LMS and British Railways Midland Region) ever used these running powers east of Hawes, or that the NER (later the LNER and British Railways Eastern Region) used them beyond Garsdale/Hawes Junction, other than for excursion traffic. The Midland section between Garsdale and Hawes was worked by block telegraph and train staff, while on the NER section there was a gradual changeover from staff and ticket to electric token working. The Midland section opened to goods traffic on 1 August 1878 and to passengers on 1 October; it was a single line and was 5¾ miles long.

The North Eastern Railway had reached Leyburn from Northallerton in 1856, and extended its line onwards from Leyburn to Askrigg from 1 February 1877; Hawes was reached in 1878. The NER operated the vast majority of services over the branch using its own motive power, with the Midland running one daily goods service into Hawes from opening and, from 1903, operating a return passenger service, known as the 'Bonnyface', between Hawes and Hellifield. This situation prevailed until April 1954, when the Eastern Region withdrew passenger services between Hawes and Northallerton (but continued with goods), the Midland Region retaining one train a day between Hawes and Garsdale stations until closure. The last train from Bradford (Forster Square) to Hawes ran on Saturday 14 March 1959 behind Stanier 2-6-4T No 42492, and passenger services were officially withdrawn two days later on the 16th and the station closed. The Eastern Region continued to run trains as far as Hawes from Northallerton for a further five years, that section of line being finally taken out of use after 27 April 1964; the last passenger working, a special charter train, had run two days earlier, though the station had been closed for some five years by then.

This section had several notable features. There was a 245-yard-long tunnel at Mossdale Head, and the four-arch, 233-foot-long, 40-foot-high Mossdale Viaduct. Around 2 miles nearer to Hawes was Appersett Viaduct, 325 feet in length and its five arches reaching 56 feet in height.

The station's yard and goods warehouse were purchased by the Yorkshire Dales National Park Authority in 1977, which offered the warehouse as premises for what is now the Dales Countryside Museum, playing a major part in establishing the site. The items that formed the basis of the Museum had started being collected as early as the 1940s by forward-thinking locals the late Marie Hartley MBE (1905-2006) and Ella Pontefract, who died in 1945, who were keen to preserve their local heritage. The items, which were catalogued by Joan Ingilby MBE and Phyllis Bentley, were by the mid-1970s in need of an adequately sized home within the area to which they were most pertinent. Finance for what was then known as the Upper Dales Folk Museum was provided by Yorkshire Museum and this, in turn, attracted grant aid from the English Tourist Board, accompanied by financial support from the Museum & Art Gallery Service for Yorkshire and Humberside. A restoration scheme for the warehouse was devised by Mr W. T. C. Walker, then the Assistant County Architect in charge of historic buildings, and a cost-effective internal layout was produced by designer Roger Simpson. A further English Tourist Board grant secured heating for the Museum, which was officially opened on 30 March 1979. The station buildings and goods warehouse were sympathetically extended in 1998 and there is now a purpose-built museum complex and a circular lecture theatre. There is also a large Tourist Information Centre and shop. The site is open daily throughout the year, except at Christmas, between 10.00am and 5.00pm. It also has a supporting organisation, the Friends of the Dales Countryside Museum, which can be accessed via the internet at *www.yorkshiredales.org.uk* or contacted via the Museum on 01969 666210.

Hawes Joint station is seen in about 1900 and in 2009. Carrying a fictional British Railways livery as No 67345 is Robert Stephenson & Hawthorns 0-6-0T No 7845 of 1955. Posed on display at the head of three Mark 1 coaches, it may perhaps be a taste of what is to come should the Wensleydale Railway achieve its long-term objective of once more running trains into Hawes from Northallerton, and onwards to connect with the Settle to Carlisle line at Garsdale. The Wensleydale Railway currently has a 99-year lease on the 22-mile stretch of trackbed between Northallerton and Redmire, with passenger services currently running between Leeming Bar, Leyburn and Redmire, a distance of nearly 17 miles. More information on this line can be found by accessing *www.wensleydalerailway.com*. Note the addition of the circular lecture theatre and museum extension in this 2009 view. *Lens of Sutton/DJW*

Hawes station is seen again looking towards Garsdale around 1900. Originally two signal boxes controlled the Joint station. Hawes West signal box was opened on 1 October 1878, being replaced by a new box from 9 September 1900; this latter structure closed on 14 April 1907. Hawes East signal box also opened on 1 October 1878, and was replaced by a new box from 12 August 1900. This became the sole signal box for the station from 14 April 1907, being renamed simply Hawes when the West box was removed and lasting until around 1959. *Lens of Sutton*

At the same location in 2009 the platform shelter is still evident on the right, and the main station buildings are intact, though hidden behind the Mark 1 coaches; the modern-day extension is apparent on the left of the picture. As with many other locations, tree growth is beginning to obscure some features, including the road overbridge. *DJW*

The last passenger train to Hawes was a Railway Travel & Correspondence Society (RCTS) special, which ran on 25 April 1964 in inclement weather conditions. Named 'The North Yorkshireman Railtour' and run by the RCTS's West Riding Branch, the train was timed to arrive at Hawes at 1.40pm and depart at 2.06pm. It featured one of the last workings of a 'B16/2' Class 4-6-0, No 61435, a 1937 Gresley rebuild of one of Vincent Raven's 'S3' Class (LNER 'B16'), built for the North Eastern Railway. No 61435 entered traffic in November 1922, was the first of seven 'B16' Class 4-6-0s to be rebuilt by Sir Nigel Gresley as a 'B16/2', and became the last member of the class to be withdrawn, in July 1964. (Gresley's successor, Edward Thompson, also rebuilt 17 members of the Class, designated 'B16/3', to different specifications.) No 61435 had previously worked the Leeds City to Harrogate leg of the railtour, and again took charge of the train at Starbeck for the trip to Hawes via Ripley, Ripon, Pickgill, Northallerton, Castle Hills Inner Junction, Ainderby, Bedale, Redmire and Aysgarth. The train, which had been strengthened at a late stage, proved too long for the loop at Hawes and had to be split to allow No 61435 to run round, as can be seen from the first picture, where the train appears to have nine coaches, split as five and four. The 'B16/2' took the train back as far as Castle Hills Inner Junction, where Gresley-designed 'V3' 2-6-2T No 67646 and Stanier-designed 2-6-4T No 42639 took over to take the train on to Middleton-in-Teesdale, which lost its passenger service in November of that year. The train was designated IZ02. *Both David J. Mitchell*

Climbing to Ais Gill

Returning to the main line to continue our journey towards Carlisle, we reach Dandry Mire (or Moorcock) Viaduct, just north of Garsdale station. Originally there were no plans for a viaduct here, but after two years of tipping material into Dandry Mire in order to create a solid base for an embankment, and two years of making little headway, the Midland Railway elected to drain the surrounding land and sink a trench in order to find solid ground on which to construct a viaduct. The result is the 50-foot-high, 227-yard-long structure seen today. It has 12 arches and 11 piers, the fourth and eighth being strengthened 'king piers'. In 1967 a Crosti-boilered 9F 2-10-0 heads a goods working northwards.

In the summer of 2008 a Leeds-Carlisle passenger service passes the same location. There has been a little modification to the dry stone walling arrangements over the intervening 41 years, but beyond that the view remains largely unaltered. *David J. Mitchell/DJW*

Preserved No 46229 *Duchess of Hamilton*, from the National Collection at York, pulls away from Dandry Mire Viaduct with a 'Cumbrian Mountain Pullman', while in the second picture we see an unusual working in the form of the yellow-liveried New Measurement Train in 2009. Introduced in 2003, the Measurement Train is made up partly of converted High Speed Train power cars and partly of Mark III coaches, and incorporates a high-speed track-recording coach and an AEA Technology Tracklab, which has a laser line scan video installed by the French company Cybernetics to detect any flaws in the railhead or the sleepers. As the train passes over any areas of track that are not up to standard, a paint spray is released, marking the particular area requiring attention so that it will be easy for engineers 'on the ground' to locate it. It also has a pantograph that can detect faults in overhead wires on electrified lines, although as the train is diesel-powered no current is drawn. The benefit of a 125mph maximum speed is that the train can integrate into timetables between service trains much more easily than could the slower measurement trains that preceded it, and it can cover the majority of the national rail network every two weeks. One of the train's three available power cars, No 43013 (the others are Nos 43014 and 43062 *John Armitt*, the latter nearest the camera in this picture and named after the former Chief Executive of Network Rail), visited Brush Traction at Loughborough in Leicestershire between March and June 2009 to be fitted with an MTU engine. *Malcolm Ranieri/David Besley*

The same train as in the previous 'past' picture is seen crossing Moorcock road bridge (constructed in 1872) in 1967, while more modern traffic, on both rail and road, is seen in 2008. There has been a recent trend towards advertising northern attractions, such as the National Railway Museum in York or Hadrian's Wall Country through pictorial advertising on the side of local trains, and this unit is similarly decorated. The building on the extreme right of the 'past' picture is Hawes Junction (or Mount Zion) Methodist Chapel, still very much in situ (see inset). It was opened in 1876, the same year in which the S&C was opened, and weekly services and a Sunday School were held here for more than a century. Although regular services no longer take place, a group named The Friends of Hawes Junction Chapel has been formed to maintain and keep it open for special events, such as the Carols by Candlelight service held each December. An extension to the rear of the building has recently been built, in keeping with the existing structure, and this was opened in August 2009. *David J. Mitchell/DJW (2)*

79

Ais Gill

The line now proceeds north through Moorcock Tunnel, over the five-arch Lunds Viaduct and on through Shotlock Hill Tunnel towards our next pictorial port of call, Ais Gill, the summit of the line at 1,169 feet above sea level. On 3 August 1963 'Jubilee' Class 4-6-0 No 45645 *Collingwood* is seen passing Ais Gill signal box heading north with a local train, with stock in the down refuge sidings. The locomotive is nearing the end of its working life, being withdrawn in October 1963 and cut up at Crewe Works in November of that year. *R. Blencowe collection*

The original signal box at Ais Gill opened on 2 August 1875 and was replaced on 26 April 1890, closing on 28 January 1981; the associated sidings were also taken out of use and removed at the same time. In the autumn of 1982 the box was moved to the Midland Railway Centre at Butterley in Derbyshire for preservation, and was commissioned at Butterley over the weekend of 8/9 September 1984. It is seen in its current location at Butterley in July 2009. *Ken Bayley*

In LMS days, 'Jubilee' No 5568 *Western Australia* approaches the summit from the north with the 'Thames-Forth Express' (later known as the 'Waverley'). No 5568 entered traffic on 25 August 1934 and was withdrawn from Newton Heath depot in April 1964.

The preserved No 46115 *Scots Guardsman* approaches the summit on Saturday 16 August 2008 at the head of a steam special carrying the 'Thames-Clyde Express' headboard. *Author's collection/DJW*

Preserved Stanier 'Coronation Pacific' No 46255 *City of Hereford* climbs towards the summit with the Stephenson Locomotive Society Midland Area's IX82 'Pennine Pacific Railtour' of Sunday 12 July 1964, scheduled to pass Ais Gill at 4.01pm. The special was worked by No 46251 from Birmingham (New Street) over Shap to Carlisle and No 46255 from Carlisle Kingmoor to Leeds City via the S&C. The train was hauled from Leeds to Crewe by 'Jubilee' Class 4-6-0 No 45647 *Sturdee* before No 46155 took over for the final return leg to Birmingham (New Street). *City of Hereford* was withdrawn from its last shed, Carlisle Kingmoor, on 30 September 1964, and had been scrapped by the end of the year. A locomotive that was first released to traffic on 31 October 1946, its career spanned less than 20 years. *RAS Marketing*

The preserved pairing of Midland Compound 4-4-0 No 1000 (piloting) and 'Jubilee' Class 4-6-0 No 5690 *Leander* is pictured hauling a heavily loaded 'Cumbrian Mountain Pullman' towards the summit on a wintry day in February 1983. *Malcolm Ranieri*

Accidents near Ais Gill
2 September 1913

The line immediately north of Ais Gill summit was the scene of one of the most serious accidents on the Settle to Carlisle line when two trains collided in the early hours of 2 September 1913. In strong wind and heavy rain, two up Scottish expresses left Carlisle for St Pancras, the first at 1.38am (scheduled departure 1.35am), the second at 1.49am. Both trains were hauled by Midland 4-4-0 locomotives. The first to leave, hauled by No 993 of the '999' Class, had a 10-coach train in tow incorporating portions from Glasgow and Stranraer, which, weighing in at 243 tons, was 13 tons above the maximum load recommended for a 4-4-0 working over Ais Gill. No pilot locomotive was available to double-head the train, and poor-quality coal hampered the engine's progress. Three miles south of Mallerstang signal box pressure dropped to 85lb (the usual pressure required was in the region of 220lb), so low that the train's vacuum brakes leaked on and the locomotive and its train ground to a standstill just below Ais Gill summit.

The following 1.49am train was much lighter, having only six coaches and weighing 157 tons. This was well within the permitted limit of 180 tons on that stretch of line for its Class '2' 4-4-0 locomotive No 446, though this was also suffering from the effects of poor coal and, allied to other problems on the footplate, including a troublesome injector, the crew's attention was sufficiently distracted for them to miss the signals at Mallerstang.

Although the driver of No 993 saw the following train fast approaching from the rear, his locomotive had insufficient pressure to move its heavy train from its standing position. The second train, travelling at around 40mph, ran into the rear of the first. In those days, as mentioned in connection with the 1910 accident near Garsdale (Hawes Junction), carriages were lit using the Pintsch system of oil-compressed gas. Hot coals from the locomotive of the second train ignited three vehicles of the first train, including a sleeping car, these being engulfed by flames as escaping gas quickly set them alight. Fourteen passengers died instantly, two more later, and a further 38 were seriously injured.

After the accident and the subsequent inquiry, the Midland Railway decided that all vehicles should now be lit using electricity rather than gas. Iron or steel loops were fitted to the outside of carriage doors to allow them to be levered open more easily in the aftermath of any accident, and shock-absorbing buffers were fitted to a large number of vehicles. Much of the timber used in new carriages was to be fireproofed, and the Midland Railway began experimenting with coaching stock utilising steel instead of wooden bodies. It could therefore be said that this accident had a far-reaching impact on the construction of coaching stock across the company's system.

31 January 1995

In addition to the events of 2 September 1913, the line near Ais Gill was the scene of a more recent accident involving two Class 156 'Sprinter' units. This occurred just before 19.00 on 31 January 1995, another dark and very wet night. A southbound Carlisle to Leeds train had to be terminated at Ribblehead due to flooding towards Settle, and had to return to Carlisle. As it headed back northwards, the 'Sprinter' ran into a landslide, which derailed both vehicles; they came to rest in darkness across both running lines, the impact having disabled all lighting but the train's headlights. Despite the driver of the next southbound train, the 17.45 Carlisle to Leeds service, seeing the headlights of the derailed unit and applying emergency braking, there was insufficient time to stop and the southbound train ploughed into the derailed train, killing its conductor and injuring 30 passengers. The official inquiry made recommendations regarding effective protection of trains in the event of accidents, improving radio communication between railway control rooms, and making more efficient use of the national radio network.

A Stanier 'Black Five' approaches Ais Gill summit with a three-coach Carlisle to Hellifield local working during the 1960s.

An English Electric Type 4 diesel locomotive, later to become known as Class 40, approaches the summit with a southbound goods working in 1965.

A modern four-car passenger equivalent passes the same spot in May 2008. Photographs of southbound trains are generally dominated by the impressive lines of Wild Boar Fell, which rises to 2,323 feet (708 metres).
R. Hewitt, Stephenson Locomotive Society/David J. Mitchell/DJW

The four-arch Ais Gill Viaduct is a popular photographic location and these two pictures were taken in very different weather conditions. In 1967, in the midst of a snowstorm, No 4498 *Sir Nigel Gresley* climbs towards the summit, while in sunshine but with storm clouds definitely gathering, No 45596 *Bahamas* makes its way south in 1989. *David J. Mitchell/Malcolm Ranieri*

On the climb towards the road overbridge near Ais Gill, a Stanier 8F 2-8-0 is captured in volcanic mode at the head of a goods train in 1967. *David J. Mitchell*

Mallerstang signal box *(inset)* is seen on 2 June 1963. This box was located in an isolated spot between Ais Gill and Kirkby Stephen and was opened on 9 September 1894, closing on 31 August 1969. A station was originally planned for this location but was never constructed. There would have been lie-by sidings here until the end of the 1950s. A service is held annually in the church at Mallerstang to commemorate those who lost their lives in the parish during the building of the line. *H. C. Casserley*

Kirkby Stephen

A Class 27 diesel approaches Kirkby Stephen West station with a northbound goods working in 1967, and preserved No 46115 *Scots Guardsman* passes the same location with a steam special carrying the 'Thames-Clyde Express' headboard in August 2008, the locomotive's first run over the S&C since restoration to full working order. The signal box it is passing is not that originally located here, but a 1970s replacement of standard BR design utilising a ground frame recovered from Kendal in the Lake District. The original box was of Midland design and was in operation between 6 May 1894 and 27 October 1974. *David J. Mitchell/DJW*

NATIONAL RAILWAY HERITAGE AWARDS

RAILWAY HERITAGE TRUST

THE RAILWAY HERITAGE TRUST
CONSERVATION AWARD
PRESENTED TO
THE SETTLE AND CARLISLE RAILWAY TRUST
FOR
KIRKBY STEPHEN STATION
BY
JOHN ARMITT
CHIEF EXECUTIVE, NETWORK RAIL
2005

'Jubilee' Class 4-6-0 No 45562 *Alberta* enters the station from the north with 'The South Yorkshireman' railtour on 7 October 1967, while in May 2008 a four-car unit, led by No 158904, arrives. The central steel girder of road underbridge No 161, seen between the running lines in the 'past' picture, was added as a strengthening measure in 1903. There would have been an angled running-in board until around 1939. The steam-era Midland-design water column has, of course, now gone; one of these was also located at the end of the southbound platform.
David J. Mitchell/DJW

'Black Five' No 44670 arrives with a northbound goods train in April 1954. The original signal box is in evidence, as is the swan-necked water column at the platform end, and the large water tank beyond the northbound platform. *H. C. Casserley*

In August 2008 both water column and tower are long gone. The signal box was replaced in 1974, and the platform lighting is much altered, though no less attractive. Although the station lost its goods facilities from 28 September 1964, the goods shed is still in situ, now used by a road haulage company, and a new footbridge has been erected, funded by the Settle-Carlisle Railway Development Company. *DJW*

The southbound 'Thames-Clyde Express' arrives at Kirkby Stephen (West) behind No 46112 *Sherwood Forester* on 26 April 1954. This train had its origins with the London, Midland & Scottish Railway (LMS), which gave the name to its express passenger departure between London (St Pancras) and Glasgow (St Enoch). The route took the train through Leicester and the East Midlands, then on to Leeds, from where it proceeded non-stop to Carlisle Citadel via the Settle to Carlisle line, and from Carlisle northwards into Scotland along the former Glasgow & South Western line to the terminus at St Enoch. The name was dropped at the outbreak of the Second World War in September 1939 and was not restored until ten years later, in September 1949, now under the auspices of British Railways (Midland Region). The service never regained the same timings it had enjoyed in the pre-war period, and in 1962 took 8hr 50min to travel between London and Glasgow. When, in 1964, the train's sister service from Edinburgh, the 'Waverley' (formerly the 'Thames-Forth Express') ceased running during the winter months, coaches for Edinburgh were added to the 'Thames-Clyde Express'. Additional stops were consequently made at several stations between Settle and Carlisle and, when Glasgow (St Enoch) closed in 1966, the service terminated at Glasgow Central. The title was last used in May 1975 on completion of the West Coast Main Line electrification programme, and the working ceased completely in the following year. *H. C. Casserley*

Kirkby Stephen West station is located approximately 1½ miles from the centre of the town that it serves. At opening, the station was known simply as Kirkby Stephen, but it was changed to Kirkby Stephen & Ravenstonedale in 1900, reverting to Kirkby Stephen in January 1935. In June 1953 it became Kirkby Stephen West, to distinguish it from Kirkby Stephen East on the line to Penrith. The name reverted to Kirkby Stephen in May 1968, just two years before the passenger service was lost on 4 May 1970; they resumed in July 1986. *DJW*

A number of subtle changes are apparent in these views from April 1954 and May 2008. The first is the addition of new lamp-posts, in a heritage style in keeping with the station, and similar in pattern to the oil lamps that would have been present on the platforms in the 1900s. A footbridge has been added and the signal box modernised, replaced by a more modern design in the 1960s. The water column is no longer there and the barrow crossing has also gone, with passengers required to cross the line by the footbridge or under the roadbridge in today's safety-conscious era. The trees behind the southbound platform now tower over the station building. *H. C. Casserley/DJW*

In the first picture the main station buildings at Kirkby Stephen are seen in around 1912. The north end of the platform has the angled running-in board, typical of the pre-Second World War period. *Lens of Sutton*

The station is seen again as it is in 2009; note the clock and floral barrels. In December 2003 the Settle & Carlisle Railway Trust was granted a 125-year lease on the station buildings. Restoration work was carried out between March and November 2004, with an official opening by HRH The Prince of Wales on Tuesday 22 March 2005. The station now has offices on both ground and first floors, a two-bedroom caretaker's flat and a meeting room, known as the Midland Railway Room, which can be hired for meetings, catering for up to 20 delegates. The project cost £241,000, which included funding from a variety of bodies, including the North West Regional Development Agency, The Railway Heritage Trust, the Friends of the Settle-Carlisle Line, the Clothworkers' Foundation and the European Regional Development Fund. In August 2009 the company Imagerail established a small shop selling light refreshments, prints and railwayana, and a Friends member has funded an automatic weather station, similar to that at Ribblehead. *DJW*

Crosby Garrett

The first picture shows Crosby Garrett station in its heyday. As much of the station was in a cutting, the main station building, on the northbound side, was located near the south end of the platform. There was a waiting shelter on each platform, both set into a recess in the embankment; that on the down side can be seen beyond the bridge. A signal box was located roughly behind the photographer, and was in operation between 16 April 1899 and 12 April 1965, though it remained available for use until 1967.

The station closed on 7 July 1952 and was demolished, but the Station Master's house, seen in the background of the 'past' picture, is still standing, though empty and undergoing refurbishment at the time this picture was taken in 2009. Decades of tree growth have obscured the view somewhat.

The third picture is the view from the bridge seen in the 'past' picture, showing the site of the platforms looking north. The recess in the wall shows where the down platform waiting shelter stood; the up platform shelter was almost directly opposite, and lasted into the 1960s, longer than the other station buildings. A landslide near this site in 1999 caused a northbound 'Sprinter' unit to become derailed, and was subsequently hit by a freight train heading south; fortunately, there were no serious injuries. *Lens of Sutton/DJW (2)*

Just south of Crosby Garrett, the railway crosses the highest structure on the line, Smardale Viaduct, which stands 130 feet high and is 237 yards long. The 12-arch structure was built between 1870 and 1875, with the last stone being laid on 8 June 1875 by Mrs Agnes Crossley, wife of the line's engineer. The Kirkby Stephen to Tebay line passed under the most northerly arch of Smardale Viaduct, and today the route is a public footpath. *DJW*

After passing the site of the former station, trains heading north pass almost immediately onto the 110-yard long, 55-foot-high, six-arch Crosby Garrett limestone viaduct, dating from 1871, then soon enter Crosby Garrett Tunnel. *DJW*

Ormside

Ormside station opened to passengers on 1 May 1876 and to goods on 1 April 1880. A signal box opened in 1876, being replaced from 11 August 1907 and closing on 8 March 1960. The station closed to goods and passengers on 2 June 1952. These views show the station in 1912 and the station building as it was in 2009. There were essentially three sizes of station on the line – small, medium and large – and this is an example of the small type. Examples of the large type are Settle and Kirkby Stephen, and of the medium type Langwathby and Lazonby. Shortly after leaving the station northbound the line crosses the 10-arch, 90-foot-high, 200-yard-long Ormside Viaduct carrying the railway over the River Eden, and heads towards Appleby-in-Westmorland. *Lens of Sutton/DJW*

Appleby-in-Westmorland

Appleby was formerly the county town of Westmorland, and when the county of Cumbria was created in 1974 the town's name was changed to Appleby-in-Westmorland in order to preserve the name of the former county for posterity. The name Appleby means 'the farmstead with apple trees' and has its origins in the Norse/Danish language, harking back to the occupation by the Vikings in the 10th century. One of the events for which the town is most famous is the Appleby Horse Fair, held at Fair Hill (formerly known as Gallows Hill), around a mile from the town, since 1685 under a charter granted by James II. Before and after the Fair the local roads and roadsides are packed with horses and caravans making their way to and from the event, as Romany families converge on Appleby to buy and sell horses and to take part in trotting and racing along Flashing Lane. The Fair runs from the first Thursday in June each year, unless it is 1 June, in which case it starts on 8 June, and lasts for one week, until the following Wednesday; it can attract up to 50,000 visitors annually. *DJW*

The station opened on 1 May 1876 and was known as Appleby until 1 September 1952, when it became Appleby West (Appleby East being the station on the Eden Valley line from Kirkby Stephen East to Penrith, part of which now forms the basis of a preservation project); it reverted to simply Appleby from 5 May 1968, Appleby East having closed to passengers on 22 January 1962 and to goods on 2 November 1964. It was one of only two stations where regular scheduled passenger trains continued to call after 4 May 1970, Settle being the other. In November 1962 'Black Five' No 44828 waits in the down platform. *J. W. T. House, C. L. Caddy collection*

Fowler 4F 0-6-0 No 44547 arrives at Appleby with a southbound goods working on 12 August 1950. The first Appleby North signal box opened on 2 August 1875 and was replaced from 26 October 1890; it can be seen beyond the down platform, but was destroyed by fire on 4 June 1951. It was replaced by a new signal box, located approximately 120 yards further north on the up side of the line on land between the junction of the Settle to Carlisle line with the North Eastern Railway's line to Appleby East. *Cooper's Railway Photographs*

The position of the 1951 replacement box can be seen in the background of the September 2008 picture, where a two-car Class 158 unit is seen waiting to continue its journey south. *DJW*

Stanier 'Black Five' 4-6-0 No 45364 passes beneath the footbridge at Appleby in this view taken from the down platform in 1954.

In May 2008 a two-car Class 158 unit is seen pulling away to continue its journey northwards. Perhaps the greatest contrast with the earlier picture, other than the motive power, is the revised station lighting. The inset shows the Midland Railway crest set into one of the Appleby station windows. *Maurice Harrison, from the Ted Hancock Collection/DJW (2)*

A Midland pairing of Nos 44898 and 46145 arrives from the north on 23 April 1960. *R. K. Blencowe collection*

In September 2008 a Freightliner coal train headed by Class 66 No 66650 passes through Appleby. The station environs are considerably more tree-lined nowadays than was the case in earlier years. The inset shows the plaque commemorating the millionth sleeper supplied to Railtrack by Corus (formerly British Steel), which was unveiled on Appleby station on 30 June 2000. *DJW (2)*

Double-headed Class 31s arrive at Appleby with what is believed to be the 09.02 from Leeds to Carlisle on 17 July 1985. The outline of the Express Dairy Company's building can just be made out in the distance; this opened in 1931 and was rail-connected, with milk tankers being dispatched south to Cricklewood, firstly as attachments to passenger trains and latterly, as traffic increased, in dedicated goods trains. (The ground frame controlling access to the dairy's sidings, released from Appleby West signal box, was taken out of use on 11 January 1970.) Workers repair the roof in a less safety-conscious age. *David J. Mitchell*

Seen from the same location (the footbridge) in 2009, note the extension to the goods shed in the form of the Appleby Training & Heritage Centre of 1996. It provides education and training courses for those interested in engineering, including a Young Engineer Programme aimed at starting young people in the engineering industry. It also specialises in contract repairs, an example of which is former Sunderland double-deck tramcar No 16, which can now be seen and ridden on at the Beamish North of England Open Air Museum. Note also the residential development beyond the station, and the installation of the splendid Midland-style lamps to replace those seen in the 1985 view. *DJW*

Appleby North Junction was where the Midland line connected with the North Eastern Railway's Eden Valley line via a spur that ran to Appleby East station, and the MR possessed running powers over the NER line to Appleby East. In turn, the NER had running powers for goods and mineral traffic over the Midland line from Appleby North Junction into Appleby West station. After the Eden Valley line closed in 1962, two sets of traffic continued to use the spur: these were trains from Merrygill/Hartley Quarry, to the east of Kirkby Stephen, until 26 June 1976, and occasional troop trains and miscellaneous goods workings to the army base at Warcop. Goods traffic from Appleby North Junction north to Petteril Bridge Junction, Carlisle, ceased when the Warcop traffic stopped, on 31 March 1989, thus removing the last goods traffic running over the line at that time.

The track between Appleby East and Warcop was never lifted following cessation of trains in 1989, and in 1995 a preservation project was started with the long-term aim of reopening the line, initially between Appleby and Warcop, with a second phase to return the line to Kirkby Stephen East, where a number of items of rolling stock are located. This is the Eden Valley Railway Trust, a Registered Charity, more details of which can be found at *www.evr.org.uk*.

In this 17 July 1985 view, a Class 25 or Class 27 runs 'wrong line' in the southbound platform with a wagon bound for Carlisle; presumably the pairing has just left the branch from Warcop and is waiting to head north.
David J. Mitchell

A second signal box formerly existed at Appleby on the other side of the track from the goods shed; it opened in 1876 and was replaced from 26 October 1886. It was known originally as Appleby, then Appleby Station from 1937 and Appleby West from 1951; it was replaced by a ground frame from 14 October 1973. The box is seen here in about 1970.
Kidderminster Railway Museum

Appleby West station is seen in April 1954, with footbridge and barrow crossing in place. Although both Kirkby Stephen and Settle now also have footbridges, Appleby was the only station on the S&C that had one installed by the Midland Railway, in 1901. *H. C. Casserley*

In 2008 the scene is still very similar, but minus the hut on the southbound platform and now sporting the elegant Midland-style lamps that are a hallmark of many of the line's stations nowadays. Refreshment trolleys, provided by the Settle-Carlisle Railway Development Company, often join the trains here. *DJW*

On 13 May 1978, while waiting to photograph a railtour hauled by preserved 9F 2-10-0 No 92220 *Evening Star*, one of Britain's best-known railway photographers, Bishop Eric Treacy MBE, suffered a fatal heart attack on the platform at Appleby station. A plaque to commemorate his memory is on the down platform. Born in London on 2 June 1907, Eric Treacy took up railway photography before the Second World War. He received an MBE for his work as an army padre during the war, afterwards becoming rector of Keighley in West Yorkshire and later, in 1949, Archdeacon of Halifax. He was Bishop of Pontefract between 1961 and 1968 and Bishop of Wakefield between 1968 and 1976. Eric Treacy believed the Settle to Carlisle railway to be one of the three main man-made wonders of the world, the others being York Minster and Hadrian's Wall; he is buried at St Kentigern's Church at Crosthwaite on the outskirts of Keswick in the Lake District. *DJW*

Appleby might seem unusual territory for a Great Western Railway locomotive *(above left)*, but it is currently home to No 4979 *Wootton Hall*, which worked on the GWR and British Railways (Western Region) for 34 years, entering service in February 1930 and being withdrawn from Oxford depot in December 1963. The loco worked in the West Country from Plymouth's Laira depot, in South Wales, when it was based at Cardiff Canton, and in the Midlands, when it was based at Tyseley in Birmingham, as well as being allocated to a number of other depots.

Like so many others, No 4979 went to Woodham Brothers' scrapyard at Barry in South Wales, from where it was rescued for preservation by the Furness Railway Trust in 1994. After a period at Lytham, the loco moved to Appleby Training & Heritage Centre on 9 March 2007 and will be restored by its owners, a Registered Charity, once sufficient funds are available. The Trust can be accessed at *www. furnessrailwaytrust.org. uk*. *DJW*

These are the current steam locomotive watering facilities at the south end of Appleby station. The reconstructed water tower was commissioned in 1991, with much of the funding being provided through the local Round Table. *DJW*

Long Marton

The next station to the north was Long Marton, built during 1875 and opened to passengers with the opening of the line on 1 May 1876. These pictures date from around 1900 and show first the station looking north from the down platform, then looking down from the bank above it; note the angled running-in board. The station closed on 4 May 1970, and at some later date British Rail arrived in the early hours of one Sunday morning and removed the platforms, taking the good stone and leaving the rest on site to the south of the station building; this event is still shrouded in mystery today. *Lens of Sutton/courtesy of David Adams*

This is Long Marton station just prior to closure, on 1 January 1970, with weed-strewn platforms (subsequently removed by British Rail), windows broken and the buildings in a generally run-down condition. The station had become an unstaffed halt on 2 January 1967, and was destined not to reopen after closure in May 1970. During the 1980s it was leased by British Rail to the North Salford High School in Manchester for holiday outings, after which it was sold privately at auction in September 1991.

In March 1993 it passed to its current owners, David and Madeleine Adams, who determinedly set about restoring it and converting it into holiday accommodation. The report of the Chartered Surveyor at the time noted that the property comprised 'seven rooms, all of which at present are unusable', which perhaps illustrates the scale of the task involved. What followed was a floor-to-ceiling renovation, including the treatment of rampant dry rot, lifting the floor, which had been covered with asphalt and concrete, refurbishing the roof and installing an upstairs, and removing and replacing the three king post trusses supporting the roof with rolled steel joists at upstairs floor, ceiling and ridge level. This work took more a decade to complete.

The third picture shows the station as it is today, fully restored and repainted in maroon and cream livery. The self-catering holiday accommodation sleeps between four and six people; the former Ladies Waiting Room has become a lounge, the Porter's Room has become the dining room, the Lamp Room the kitchen, and the former Ladies Toilet is now the bathroom. Two upstairs bedrooms, a double and a twin, have been added. Original fittings have been used wherever possible, failing which exact replicas have been made in the style of the originals. For more information on staying at Long Marton station, call David and Madeleine Adams on 0161 775 5669 or visit www.longmartonstation.fsnet.co.uk. *Courtesy of David Adams (2)/DJW*

The first view, from about 1900, shows the station looking towards Appleby. In earlier days, an aerial ropeway transported buckets containing barytes from a nearby mine to the station yard, where it was dropped into hopper wagons and taken on by rail.

The 2009 view shows the station building as it is now, together with new fencing and one of the grassed areas that have been created. When restoration began the station building was largely hemmed in by tree growth, which had to be cleared, as it was both cutting out the light and threatening to damage the retaining wall over the road. *Courtesy of David Adams/DJW*

In the spring of 2008 Freightliner Class 66 No 66566 makes its way north from Long Marton past Kirkby Thore with coal empties heading for Scotland. Coal traffic is the most prolific freight transported over the Settle to Carlisle route, and sees Scottish and imported coal, which is lower in sulphur than English coal, transported southwards to English power stations.

In the background is the plasterboard factory of British Gypsum, the industry that, with coal, represents the lion's share of freight traffic over the Settle and Carlisle line. Gypsum is a naturally occurring rock, which, when ground into a powder and heated, loses most of its moisture. It is then mixed with water and forms a paste or 'slurry', which sets solid. This has made gypsum an extremely useful building material and forms the basis of a huge industry producing a wide range of building products. In recent years, high-quality synthetic gypsum, produced primarily by a process that removes sulphur dioxide from power station flue gases (desulphogypsum) has become available to supplement the supplies of mined products, and this substance is among the materials transported over the S&C to Kirkby Thore. English, Welsh & Scottish Railway took over this traffic from Transrail and, since 2003, GB Railfreight (now First GBRf) has taken on some of these workings, emanating from West Burton Power Station in Nottinghamshire. This followed a trial run in September 2002 when GBRf moved 20,000 tonnes of imported desulphurised gypsum (DSG) from Hull Docks, where it was loaded at Hull Bulk Handling Terminal, to Kirkby Thore. The Gypsum Works has manufactured Thistle plasters since 1910, and plasterboard since the 1960s.

      The stretch of line passing Kirkby Thore was the subject of major engineering works in 2009, resulting in the line being closed for 18 days between late on 8 July and early on 28 July. There had been a permanent speed restriction in place near the Gypsum Works since the early 1970s, largely due to mine workings beneath the track, and work on three bridges together with the relaying of a mile-long stretch of line was necessary in order to raise the line running speed to facilitate the smoother passage of freight workings using the route – as well as ensuring that no harm came to a colony of great crested newts that resided nearby! The investment of several million pounds in the infrastructure here is another sign of the renewed importance attached to the Settle to Carlisle line as a freight route. *DJW*

Culgaith

Culgaith station opened on 1 April 1880. Originally, no station had been planned by the Midland Railway at this location, but the intervention of the local clergyman at the time of the line's construction, Rev G. W. Atkinson, saw the MR agree to provide a station on condition that the local authority provided road access to it. The 'past' picture shows the station in its original form, with the first signal box, opened in 1880. The southbound platform was of timber construction; another unusual feature was the down side station building itself, different from any other on the line. *Lens of Sutton*

In 2009 the station is a private residence, with the former crossing keeper's cottage adjacent to it. Passenger services ceased here on 4 May 1970 and never resumed. *DJW*

The original Culgaith signal box of 1880 was replaced with a new one on 4 October 1908. This building is still in use, though the crossing gates gave way to a manned barrier in 1976. *Lens of Sutton/DJW*

The station had a goods yard at the north end on the opposite side of the line from the signal box, though no goods shed was ever provided. The station lost its goods facilities from 5 October 1964. This view shows the up platform and the adjacent creamery. *H. C. Casserley*

Langwathby

A War Department 'Austerity' Class 2-8-0 No 90496 passes through Langwathby at the head of a short southbound goods working. *J. W. T. House, C. L. Caddy collection*

Today, as a southbound train calls led by single-car Class 153 No 153360, much of the background is obscured behind trees, and the telegraph poles, in common with much of the rest of the line, are long gone. However, the location of the underbridge (though modified) and the curve of the track are still as they were. The steel centre girder of the bridge was added by the Midland Railway as a strengthening measure in 1903-04. A new shelter, on the left, has been provided for use by passengers waiting for northbound trains, since the main station building has become a cafe restaurant. The station is used by more than 20,000 passengers per year. *DJW*

The station opened to goods and passengers on Monday 1 May 1876 as Longwathby, but the name was changed to Langwathby from 1st October of that year. It is seen here around 1972, looking north towards Carlisle; by this time the station had closed to both goods and passenger traffic. *Lens of Sutton*

In the summer of 2008 the station is clearly in a better state of health and much less neglected. A signal box was located here and was in operation when the line opened for goods traffic on 2 August 1875, though the station itself did not open to either until 1 May 1876. The box's original name was Long Wathby Station, changing to Longwathby, then Langwathby. The original was replaced from 5 July 1903 and this later structure was taken out of use from 27 October 1968. There was also a signal box at Staingill to the south, between Langwathby and Culgaith; this opened on 2 August 1875 and had closed by the end of 1880. *DJW*

This pre-Grouping view, thought to date from around 1912, shows the station in the heyday of the Midland Railway. It closed to goods from 6 July 1964 and to passengers from 4 May 1970, reopening on a weekend basis during the summer from 1976 onwards in connection with the second season of Dales Rail workings; it reopening permanently from 14 July 1986. *Lens of Sutton*

The 'present' view shows the station in September 2008, including the 'new' up platform waiting shelter, in a similar position to the one it replaced. *DJW*

The station building at Langwathby has now been converted into the popular Brief Encounter cafe and restaurant. Independent of Northern Rail, the cafe was established by Anthony and Sandra Henderson in 2001, winning the Railtrack Award in the National Railway Heritage Awards in the same year. Piped water and electric lighting had to be installed in place of paraffin lamps, and the stone flags of the Waiting Room had to be rebedded. The former Ladies Waiting Room has become the kitchen, its fireplace being moved into the Ticket Office, while the Ticket Office has become a dining area. In addition to providing morning coffee, light lunches, afternoon teas and Sunday roasts, the cafe also sells a range of pictures, cards, cakes, chocolate and biscuits. The pictures show the station building in which the cafe is located, the 'new' Waiting Room, which is now an extended dining area, and the plaque commemorating the 2001 award. Information on opening can be obtained on 01768 881902. The station drive is also home to the Cars of Distinction wedding car hire company. *All DJW*

Little Salkeld

Little Salkeld station opened to goods and passenger services on 1 May 1876, closing to goods on 6 July 1964 and to passengers on 4 May 1970. The signal box opened on 2 August 1875 and was replaced by the structure pictured here from 13 August 1899; it closed after the station lost its goods facilities. *Lens of Sutton*

Today, both the station building and the Station Master's house are in private ownership, with the platforms still remaining. The main station building on the up platform is seen on 27 December 1985. *Stephenson Locomotive Society*

Shortly after passing the site of Little Salkeld station, the line crosses the seven-arch Little Salkeld Viaduct, spanning Briggle Beck. The structure, built in 1874-1875, is 60 feet high and 134 yards long. The nearby village is home to Cumbria's only working watermill, which dates from 1745. *DJW*

Accidents at Little Salkeld

Three accidents occurred in and around Little Salkeld over the years, of varying levels of severity. The first took place on 19 January 1918, around three-quarters of a mile north of the station in Long Meg cutting, and involved the northbound express to Glasgow, which had left St Pancras station at 8.50am. There was no element of human error on this occasion, just nature taking its course. A platelayer walking through the cutting around 5 minutes prior to the train reaching the spot had seen nothing amiss, yet as the train entered the cutting it ploughed into a huge landslide, which covered the track with debris, at a speed of 60mph. The locomotive, 4-4-0 No 1010, ended up on its side and the two leading carriages were badly damaged, with seven passengers being killed.

The second accident, on 10 July 1933, also involved No 1010, which, while heading a southbound passenger express, collided with wagons being propelled into the station siding by a goods locomotive. The accident occurred as a result of the signalman at Little Salkeld omitting to check with the boxes on either side of the station whether any other trains were in the area. The driver of the goods train was killed, and considerable damage was sustained by the passenger stock.

No 1010 (originally No 1005 prior to the 1907 Midland Railway renumbering) was built at Derby in 1905, one of a batch numbered between 1005 and 1014 constructed between October and December of that year. It was one of the famous 'Compound' locomotives, designed by Richard Deeley (1855-1944), who replaced Samuel Johnson as Chief Mechanical Engineer to the Midland Railway on 1 January 1904. It was the greater weight of the Compound locomotives that led to many bridges, including several on the Settle to Carlisle line (mentioned elsewhere), needing to be strengthened in the early years of the 20th century. No 1010 survived into British Railways service, though was not allocated a BR number, being withdrawn in July 1949.

The third accident occurred in 1961 with the derailment of a northbound goods to the north of the station, which was subsequently hit by a southbound goods train.

Long Meg Sidings

The signal box at the site of Long Meg Sidings, between Little Salkeld and Lazonby & Kirkoswald, is still in place today, its condition gradually deteriorating. The sidings served a mine, which was rail-connected from 1896, when a Midland Railway signal box controlled the line. The mine and the box closed in 1915, but reopened in 1922 when the Long Meg Plaster & Mineral Company Limited (British Plaster Board Limited from 1939, later part of British Gypsum) was formed to mine anhydrite. A ground frame controlled access to the sidings until the mid-1950s, but a new signal box was opened on 3 July 1955 and remained operational until 1983, although the mine closed on 31 January 1976. The signal box was last used on 17 November 1983 in connection with diverted traffic from the West Coast Main Line. Until its closure the site yielded 5 million tons of anhydrite, mainly for use in the manufacture of sulphuric acid and fertilisers, and much of it transported by rail. In September 2009 a southbound Class 155 unit approaches the derelict signal box; the train will shortly cross the seven-arch Eden Lacy (Long Meg) Viaduct, built between 1871 and 1875, 137 yards long and 60 feet high. *DJW*

The mine had its own steam locomotives for shunting, which worked wagons either to the plaster mill or down to the main line. The last of these was *W. S. T.*, an Andrew Barclay 0-4-0ST built in 1954 and delivered to the Long Meg site on 10 June of that year. The name is the initials of William Steuart Trimble, the Deputy Chairman of the plaster company. The loco remained at Long Meg until 1969, when it was transferred to the company's nearby Cocklake Works to act as spare engine to the site's then recently introduced fleet of diesels. In 1980

British Gypsum, which by now owned the Cocklake Works, sought a new home for the locomotive. This caused considerable interest, and eventually *W. S. T.* found a new home at the Bowes Railway, Springwell Village, Tyne and Wear, where it arrived on 7 May 1981. Initially based at Bowes on long-term loan, it has now been placed permanently with the Bowes Railway. It has been restored to its original olive green livery and is pictured at Bowes, with driver John Young in charge, in September 2008. Details of Bowes Railway opening times can be found by calling 0191 416 1847.

Also preserved is *W. T. T.*, named after William Tennant Trimble, father of WST. This is also an Andrew Barclay 0-4-0ST, No 2134 built in 1942, which has been privately preserved at Carnforth since 1971. *DJW*

Lazonby & Kirkoswald

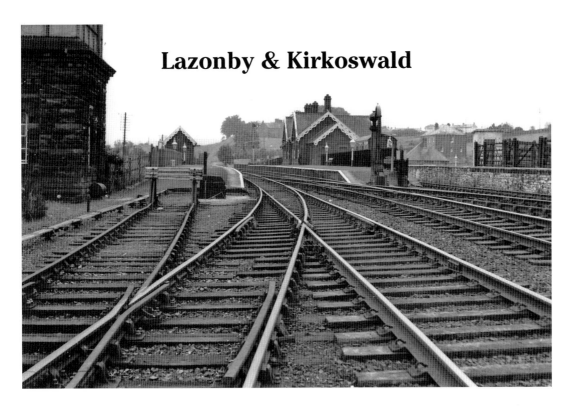

Lazonby & Kirkoswald station is seen looking south in the 1960s and in May 2009. Apart from the main running lines, all of the other tracks and connections have been removed, though both up and down platforms remain; they were in use on an occasional basis from the summer of 1976, and permanently from 16 July 1986. Note the 'bus shelter'-style waiting facility on the northbound platform, provided because the main station building is now in private commercial use. *Lens of Sutton*

In the 1960s view the cattle dock, heavily used in previous years, is still standing. The station lost its goods facilities from 2 November 1964, and the down side connections to the goods yard were decommissioned from 29 March 1965. *DJW*

A wooden signal box was located at Lazonby, opening on 19 July 1895 and closing on 25 June 1969 (or according to some sources 12 April 1965). This replaced an original signal box dating back to the opening of the line to goods traffic on 2 August 1875. The box stood just to the north of the water tank on the up side, behind the photographer in the 'past' picture on the previous page. This undated view shows the 1895 signal box.

Just south of the station is the 99-yard long Lazonby Tunnel, constructed during 1871 and 1872, at the south end of which was a sand siding, connected to the up main line and worked by a one-lever ground frame, released by an Annett's Key from Lazonby signal box. (An Annett's Key is a large key used to lock/unlock signalling apparatus; it takes its name from J. E. Annett of the London, Brighton & South Coast Railway, who patented his design in 1875.) The siding was taken out of use from 28 July 1963. *Kidderminster Railway Museum*

A southbound train arrives in the spring of 2009. The station was initially known as Lazonby until July 1895, when it became Lazonby & Kirkoswald. In common with many others on the line, it became an unstaffed halt on 2 January 1967 and closed to passengers on 4 May 1970, reopening on 16 July 1986, although Dales Rail trains had called at the station at weekends during the summer months since 1976. *DJW*

The station had a goods shed that could accommodate three wagons. It was an extremely busy facility during the steam era, particularly for the transport of livestock with, at its peak, an average of 2,435 wagon loads of livestock leaving the station in the period 1916-1922. Though the station lost its goods facilities more than 40 years ago, the goods shed is still in situ as the reception building for Bells of Lazonby, which was established as a one-man bakery business in 1946 by the current Managing Director's father; it now has five shops and is a supplier to other local stores. The station building is now home to Bells Business Centre. *Both DJW*

The Station Master's house is still standing, now in private ownership, and the Midland Hotel is handily placed, adjacent to the station at Lazonby. Keen-eyed readers will note that there is more than a touch of Great Western influence incorporated into the sign! *Both DJW*

Incident at Griseburn

On the night of 29 November 1948 a 50-ton breakdown crane that had run away at Griseburn, some 23 miles away finally came to rest at Lazonby. Some wagons were being rerailed at Griseburn, but in between the task being completed and the crane being attached to the works train for its return home, the brakes were not fully secured and a gentle nudge from the locomotive was enough to send the crane, its jib unsecured, rolling downhill towards Carlisle. As with many other incidents on the line, this took place during the hours of darkness, which made effecting a rescue much more difficult. One man was killed and two more were injured as they attempted to stop the crane.

Armathwaite

Heading north from Lazonby the line crosses the nine-arch Armathwaite Viaduct, 80 feet high and 176 yards long, and passes through the 325-yard-long Armathwaite Tunnel before arriving at Armathwaite station, seen here looking north towards Carlisle. Opened to passengers on 1 May 1876 with the opening of the line, it was closed to passengers on 4 May 1970, reopening in July 1986. The station closed to goods traffic on 6 April 1964. *Lens of Sutton*

The signal box at the north end of the station, opened on 16 July 1899 and operational until 15 January 1983, has been externally restored and painted into its former Midland Railway colours by volunteers from the Friends, while the goods shed is now in private domestic ownership. Note the somewhat truncated chimneys on the station building today, as compared to the earlier view. Today Armathwaite is the last stop on the line before Carlisle Citadel. *DJW*

Low House Crossing

Between Armathwaite and the former Cotehill station site the line crosses Dry Beck Viaduct of seven arches, 80 feet high and 139 yards long. After this, the line soon reaches the second of the two level crossings on the line, at Low House, seen first in about 1970.

The crossing gates gave way to barriers in 1975, and the location is seen again in 2009, the barriers just descending prior to the passage of a train. Just north of Low House is the four-arch High Stand Gill/Cotehill/Knothill Viaduct and the site of the former Cotehill Station, closed on 7 April 1952 and subsequently demolished. *Kidderminster Railway Museum/DJW*

Cumwhinton

Cumwhinton station opened on 1 May 1876 and closed to goods and passengers on 5 November 1956. Its signal box was in operation from 2 August 1875, when the line first opened to goods traffic, and was replaced in 1897; the replacement structure, seen on the up side of the line in the background, was in operation until 1 March 1958. This general view from the steam era shows the station buildings and extremely well-kept gardens with signal box and sidings visible directly to the north of the platforms.

In addition to the main station building, both the Station Master's house and Midland Railway workers' cottages are still in existence as private residences. *Professor Fordyce, Lens of Sutton/DJW*

Beyond Cumwhinton to the north lies Scotby station, closed on 1 February 1942, which for many years could claim to be the Midland Railway's most northerly station; the yard has been sold for housing, but the Station Master's house and station building live on in private ownership.

Carlisle Citadel

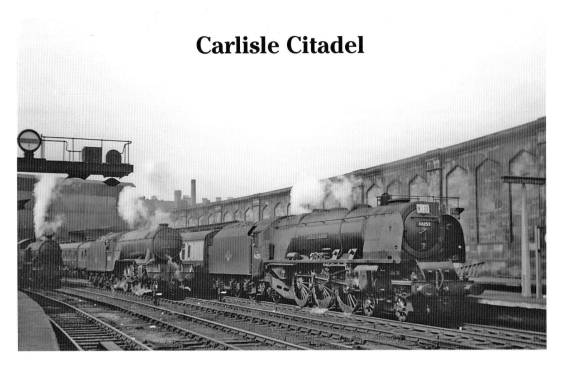

Carlisle Citadel is our final destination. The station dates from 1847, though it was extensively rebuilt during 1875 and 1876. Its imposing facade was designed by Sir William Tite, whose other designs include the Bank of England and the Royal Exchange buildings in London. An interesting array of motive power is seen on 19 July 1959, with No 46253 *City of St Albans* at the head of an up express, with Gresley-designed 'V2' Class 2-6-2 No 60802 on the adjacent road. *RAS Marketing*

Electrified since the mid-1970s, Carlisle station is seen again with a 'Pendolino' unit heading south for Birmingham (New Street). *DJW*

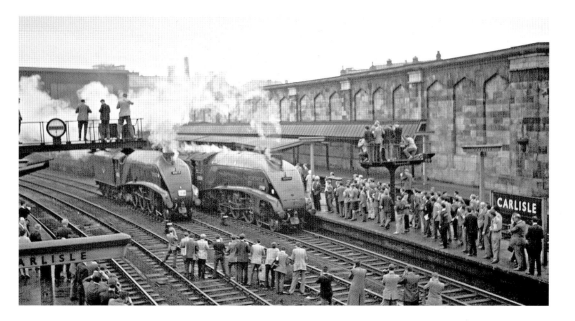

One look at this remarkable picture is enough to imagine health & safety officers the length and breadth of the country being loaded screaming into the back of ambulances suffering from acute shock! The date is 30 June 1963, the occasion the Railway Correspondence & Travel Society's 'Three Summits Railtour' organised by the RCTS's West Riding Branch. The 'A4' 'Pacifics' are Nos 60004 *William Whitelaw* (*Great Snipe* prior to July 1941) and 60023 *Golden Eagle*. The ten-coach train started at Leeds City South, with No 60023 in charge, working on only one injector for much of the outward trip; at Carlisle Stanier 'Pacific' No 46255 *City of Hereford* took the train on to Carstairs via Beattock. At Carstairs 'Jones Goods' No 103 and No 57581 headed the train to Auchinleck, with No 60004 bringing the train southwards via Dumfries to Carlisle. It is at this point that the picture was taken, with No 60004 having arrived from Auckinleck and No 60023 waiting to take the train southwards on the last leg of the railtour to Leeds City South via Penrith and Shap. The time is just after 7.00pm. *David J. Mitchell*

In May 2009 we see the more mundane scene of a Carlisle to Leeds train (on the right) awaiting departure. *DJW*

The shed for Settle to Carlisle locomotives was originally that at Durran Hill. Built on a site of around 28 acres near the junction between the Midland and North Eastern lines, the roundhouse had a 55-foot turntable inside, with a 60-foot turntable outside and space to house and service 24 locomotives. This shed closed on 16 February 1936, reopening temporarily in 1943 and finally closing again, permanently, in the late 1950s, being demolished in 1964.

When Durran Hill closed for the second time, in 1959, Carlisle Kingmoor provided locomotives for the Settle to Carlisle route at its northern end, Leeds Holbeck (20A) fulfilling that role at the southern end of the line; the latter closed to steam from 2 October 1967. Kingmoor was the former Caledonian Railway shed, opened in 1874 to service locomotives working on the Carlisle to Glasgow main line. It passed into LMS and later British Railways ownership before closing in 1968, when it gave way to a purpose-built diesel depot nearby. Here No 45562 *Alberta* is pictured on shed prior to a turn over the S&C in 1967. Built by the North British Locomotive Company in Glasgow in 1934, *Alberta* was a Leeds Holbeck locomotive at the time of this picture, the shed from which it was withdrawn on 31 October 1967; a favourite with enthusiasts during the final years of British Railways main-line steam, the loco was scrapped on 31 May 1968.

From 1987 the Kingmoor sidings site was developed into a nature reserve, which is home to a number of species of wild flowers. Today's Carlisle Kingmoor Traction Maintenance Depot for servicing diesel locomotives is located on the opposite side of the West Coast Main Line from the former steam shed. The 'new' facility was opened in January 1968 but closed by British Rail in 1987. The site was revived by the rail company DRS (Direct Rail Services) in 2000 as a base for its main-line locomotives, formerly serviced at Sellafield in Cumbria. DRS was created by British Nuclear Fuels Limited, later being transferred to the Nuclear Decommissioning Authority in 2005, and among many other types of traffic handles nuclear flask trains throughout England. *David J. Mitchell*

Although a little frivolous, it would have been a shame not to compare two locomotives carrying the name *City of Carlisle*! The first is the handsome Stanier 'Pacific' No 46238, seen at Skipton being prepared prior to working an RCTS/SLS 'North Eastern' railtour over the S&C to Carlisle. This was day one of a five-day railtour and started at York, travelling via the Derwent Valley Light Railway to Selby, Wetherby, Harrogate, Ilkley and Skipton prior to the journey to Carlisle; the date is 29 September 1963. *David J. Mitchell*

The 2009 version of *City of Carlisle* is seen at its home station, perhaps lacking the grace of its forerunner, but with a nicely planted-out tender! *DJW*

Index of locations